*Get Started*

# Growing Vegetables

Get Started

# Growing Vegetables

LONDON, NEW YORK, MUNICH,
MELBOURNE, DELHI

**Project Editor** Becky Shackleton
**Project Art Editor** Gemma Fletcher
**Senior Editor** Alastair Laing
**Managing Editor** Penny Warren
**Managing Art Editor** Alison Donovan
**Senior Jacket Creative** Nicola Powling
**Jacket Design Assistant** Rosie Levine
**Pre-production Producer** Sarah Isle
**Producer** Jen Lockwood
**Art Directors** Peter Luff, Jane Bull
**Publisher** Mary Ling

**DK Publishing**
**North American Consultant** Lori Spencer
**Editor** Kate Johnsen
**Senior Editor** Rebecca Warren

**DK India**
**Editors** Suefa Lee, Vibha Malhotra
**Managing Editor** Alka Thakur Hazarika
**Art Editors** Prashant Kumar, Karan Chaudhary
**Deputy Managing Art Editor** Priyabrata Roy Chowdhury

**Written by** Simon Akeroyd

First American Edition, 2013

Published in the United States by DK Publishing,
375 Hudson Street, New York, New York 10014

10 9 8 7 6 5 4 3 2 1
001—188215—Jan/2013



Published in Great Britain by Dorling Kindersley Limited.

A catalog record for this book is available from the Library of Congress.

ISBN 978-1-4654-0196-0



Printed and bound by Leo Paper Products Ltd, China



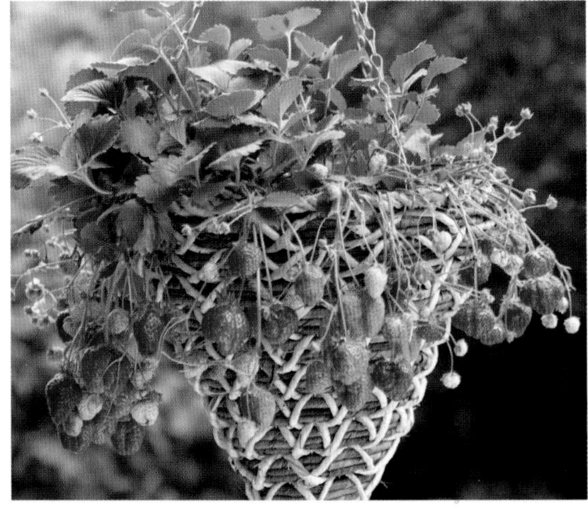

# Contents

Build Your Plan 6 • Essential Equipment 8 • Potting Mix and Soil Types 12
Preparing Your Soil 15 • Growing Locations 16 • Choosing a Site 18
**The Science of...** The Life Cycle of Plants 20 • Photosynthesis 22 • Plant Needs 24

## 1 Start Simple

SOW SEEDS 28
PLANT OUT 30
WATER YOUR PLANTS 32
TIE IN AND PINCH OFF 34

**Salad in a Window Box 36**
Lettuce and Edible Flowers 40
Spinach and Swiss Chard 41
**Tomatoes in a Pot 42**
Herbs in a Pot 46
Roots in a Pot 47
**Herbs in a Basket 48**
**Onions from Sets 52**
**Garlic 56**
**Strawberries in a Basket 60**
Tumbling Tomatoes 65
BASIC PLANT CARE 66
PROTECT PLANTS FROM SLUGS 67
FEED 68
WEED 69

## 2 Build On It

SOW IN FURROWS AND THIN OUT 72
REPOT 73
HARDEN OFF AND PROTECT FROM COLD 74
MULCH 76
STAKE 77

**Potatoes in a Tub 78**
**Zucchini in a Bag 82**
Pumpkins and Large Squashes 86
Winter and Summer Squashes 87
**Peppers in a Pot 88**
Sweet Corn 93
**Carrots in a Bag 94**
Turnips and Beets 98
Parsnips 99
**Cabbage 100**
Broccoli 105
**Beans up a Tepee 106**
Peas 111
**Fall Raspberries 112**
**Plant an Apple Tree in a Pot 116**
Plant a Fig Tree in a Pot 121
**Black Currants 122**
White and Red Currants 126
Gooseberries 127

PROTECT PLANTS FROM PESTS 128

## 3 Take It Further

PLANNING A KITCHEN GARDEN 132
CROP ROTATION 134
MAKE COMPOST AND LEAF MOLD 136

**Leeks 138**
**Eggplant 144**
**Asparagus 150**
**Globe Artichokes 154**
**Create an Herb Parterre 158**
**Blueberries in a Pot 164**
Strawberries in a Container 168
Plant a Pear Tree in a Pot 169
**Plant a Plum Tree 170**
Plant a Cherry Tree 175
BASIC PRUNING 176
PRUNING SHAPES 180
**Store Carrots in Soil 182**
Store Crops 184

Index 188
Acknowledgments 192

# Build Your Plan

This book is divided into three sections: Start Simple, Build On It, and Take It Further. These chapters are carefully structured to help you learn new skills and techniques and then apply your increasing knowledge by completing the 22 projects.

**Getting Started**

You can grow crops whether you have a large yard or just a window box, but the key to success is understanding your site before you start. The introduction to this book guides you through different soils and potting mixes, shows you where you can sow and plant, and tells you how to prepare your soil. It also shows you the equipment you'll need to keep your plants healthy.

**Planting Symbols**

These symbols indicate what growing conditions your plant needs: sunshine or shade, or moist or light soil.

*These are given at the start of each project*

**full sun**

**moist soil**

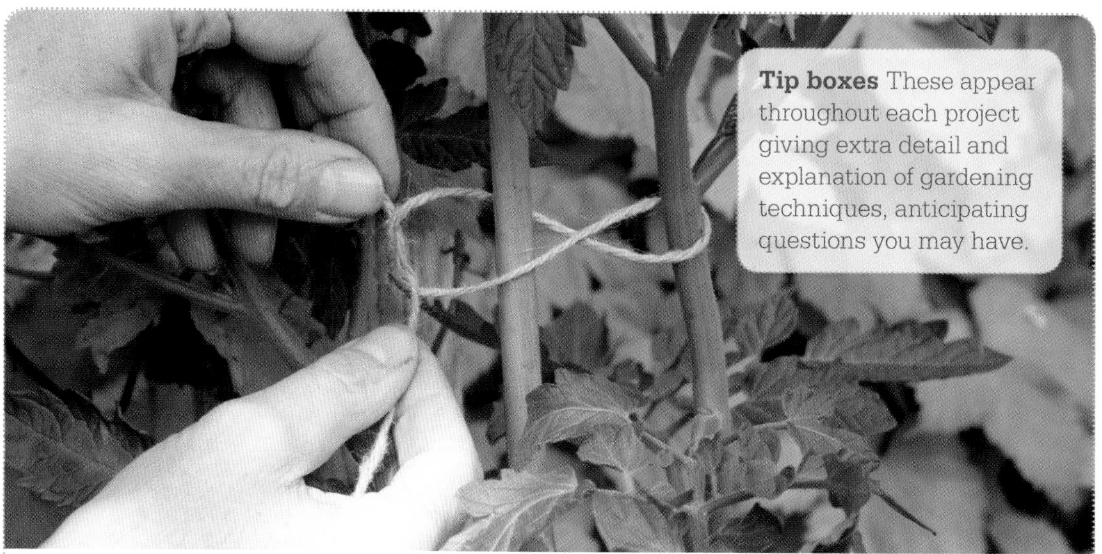

**Tip boxes** These appear throughout each project giving extra detail and explanation of gardening techniques, anticipating questions you may have.

## Key Techniques

At the beginning and end of each section are the techniques you'll need to know so that you can complete your projects successfully. They range from learning how to sow seeds and repot seedlings to planning your own kitchen garden and making compost.

**1** In every project, illustrated step-by-step text guides you carefully through the process of sowing, planting, nurturing, and harvesting your crops. The text explains in detail exactly how you need to care for your plants.

**Careful!** To guide you and give further useful advice, key information about each step is flagged, preventing you from making common mistakes.

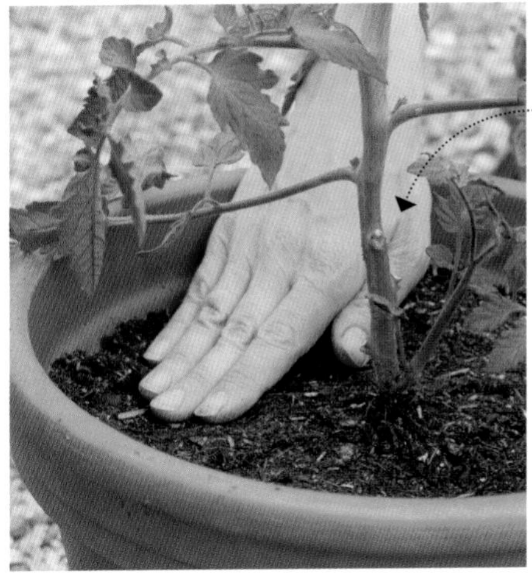

*Details about each task are pointed out*

## Caring for your **Plants**

These handy boxes are filled with troubleshooting tips and ongoing care advice so that you can keep your crops healthy and productive as they grow.

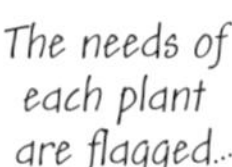
The needs of each plant are flagged

*Caption tells you when your crop will be ready to harvest*

### Things to watch out for...

**The "Care" boxes** appear at the end of each project and list the key problems that the crop might face, whether that be a tendency to attract slugs and snails or a need for constantly moist soil. Practical advice is given to help you prevent or resolve these problems. This box also contains any other relevant information relating to the care of your plant, such as harvesting or pruning.

**Now turn the page to find out more ▸▸▸**

# Essential **Equipment**

**MUST-HAVE TOOLS**

*Although growing your own crops isn't difficult, there are a few pieces of equipment that every gardener needs, such as a watering can and trowel. Invest in the best-quality tools you can afford—not only will they last well over time, but they will be a pleasure to use every time you step into your garden.*

**Watering can**
*The fine nozzle distributes the flow of water so that it doesn't damage young, delicate seedlings*

**Dibber**
*Used to create planting holes, a dibber is pushed into the soil to the appropriate depth*

**Hand fork**
*This tool allows you to be more precise when digging weeds and lifting plants than if using a large fork*

**Spade**
*Essential for lifting and moving soil or mulches and digging grit or soil in*

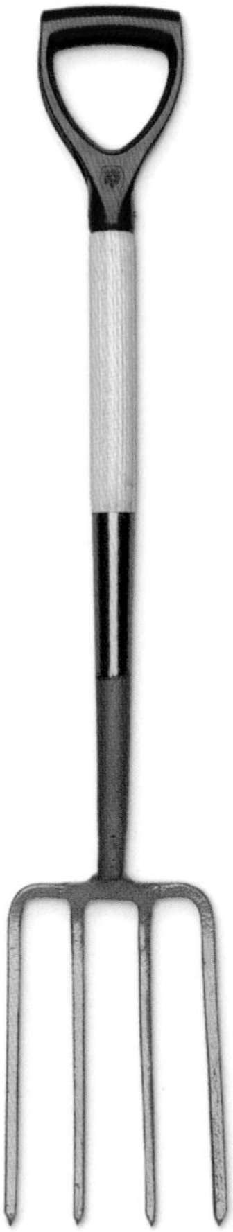

**Fork**
*Lift weeds, turn the soil over, and harvest root crops using a long-handled fork*

**Trowel**
*Create neat planting holes in the soil with this tool and use to harvest crops such as garlic*

**Hoe**
*Use to weed around your crops by lifting the soil and chopping through weeds. Long-handled types are also available*

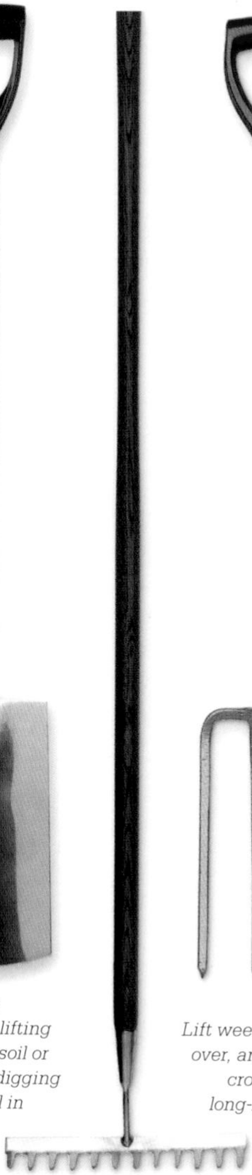

**Rake**
*Use this tool to level the soil and break it down to a fine texture before sowing and planting*

**Gloves**
*Protect your hands when using fertilizers or insecticides and when pruning thorny plants*

**Drill**
*Use to create drainage holes in pots and attach sturdy brackets for hanging baskets*

**Scissors**
*Use to harvest cut-and-come-again salad crops and snip garden twine to size*

**Pruners**
*The sturdy blades are essential for pruning fruiting shrubs and trees and harvesting crops with woody stems*

**Seed Markers**
*Mark your pots and rows with these so that you don't get your seedlings mixed up*

**Utility knife**
*Use this sharp blade to create clean-cut planting holes when laying weed-suppressing fabrics*

**Asparagus knife**
*The curved sharp blade of this tool makes it useful for harvesting the spears of asparagus close to ground level*

**Tape measure**
*Essential for ensuring that your seedlings have enough space between them*

## ESSENTIAL EXTRAS

**Poles and twine**
*Support tall or top-heavy plants by tying them to sturdy stakes or poles*

**Tree stake and tie**
*Use a stake and tie to keep fruit trees upright—the extendable ties give the trunks room to grow*

# Essential **Equipment** *continued*

## CONTAINERS

*From small plastic pots that can be kept warm on a window ledge while seeds germinate to large, cold-proof tubs for fruit trees, there are containers to suit your crops at all stages of growth. Just make sure they have holes in the bottom and place crocks in the base to help with drainage.*

**Window box**
*These enable you to grow crops on a windowsill so that they are easy to harvest. A range of styles is available*

**Terra-cotta pots**
*These attractive pots make a lovely garden feature, but are porous and drain fairly quickly*

**Plastic pots**
*Cheap and cheerful, these pots are ideal for seed sowing and are available in a range of sizes*

**Seed flats**
*Sow seeds in the compartments or cells of these trays so that the seedlings are easy to move once they develop*

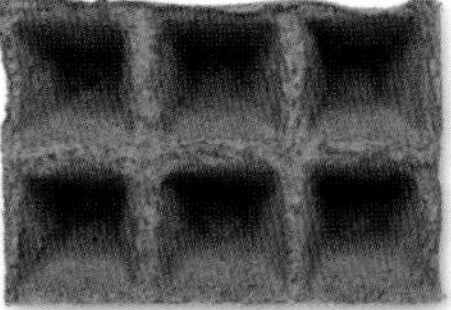

**Biodegradable pots and cell packs**
*Sow seeds in these and once the plants begin to grow, plant the pots into the ground—this removes the need to lift plants and risk disturbing their roots*

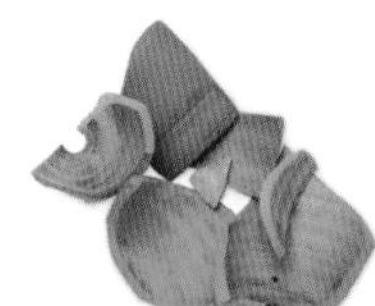

**Crocks**
*Place pieces of terra-cotta in the bottom of containers to help the soil to drain*

**Tote**
*Use a deep container for root crops or large plants—totes, bins, or planting bags make great growing locations*

**Bracket**

**Hanging basket**
*Create a hanging display of crops in a basket that is attached to a sturdy surface, such as a wall or fence*

## EXTRA HELP

*Sometimes your crops may need a bit of extra help and protection if temperatures drop or weeds and pests threaten, while some tender crops such as peppers won't even consider germinating unless you give them a warm environment after sowing. These essential items will make it easy for you to keep crops healthy and happy as they grow.*

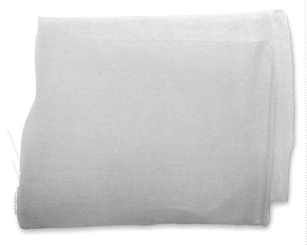

**Netting**
*Use netting anchored at the base of plants to keep out large pests such as birds. Finer, insect-proof mesh will protect plants from pests such as cabbage white butterflies*

**Fabric**
*If frost is threatened, use horticultural fabric to protect tender plants or the blossoms of plum and cherry trees from damage—simply lay it over your crops*

**Black landscape fabric**
*This fabric can be laid on the ground before planting—it helps to warm the soil, control weed growth, and retain soil moisture. Cut holes and plant your crops through it*

**Propagator**
*A propagator provides a warm environment for seeds that need higher temperatures to germinate, and young seedlings. Choose heated models or simple plastic structures*

# Potting mix and soil types

To be successful in the vegetable garden, you need to provide suitable growing conditions for your crops: the soil must contain enough nutrients and drain well. Ideal conditions vary from crop to crop, but there is a wide range of potting mixes that can be used for plants in pots. If your soil is heavy or very sandy, you can improve it by digging in compost or well-rotted manure.

## General-purpose potting mix

General-purpose potting mix is a useful soil improver and can be dug into your soil to improve its bulk and ability to retain moisture. It can also be used in containers, hanging baskets, or even for seed sowing, but is prone to drying out quickly. There are a number of different types, containing varying ratios of peat, soil, sand, and fertilizers, so read the instructions and choose the one that will best support the plants you want to grow.

## Propagation mix

Propagation mix is often soil-based, making it heavier than general-purpose potting mix and much better at retaining moisture. Its fine texture makes it ideal for seed sowing, either in individual pots or in cell packs. Propagation mix does contain some nutrients, but in fairly low quantities, which suits emerging seedlings in the early stages of development. Some companies also produce mixes for repotting and pricking out.

## Acidic potting mix

This mix has a low pH, making it suitable for crops that thrive in acidic conditions, such as blueberries and cranberries. It can either be added to raised or sunken beds to increase the acidity of the existing soil or used to fill containers. Like general-purpose potting mix, it can quickly dry out and will need watering regularly if in containers. Take care to water this mix using rainwater because regular tap water will alter its pH.

Clay soils have a fudgelike texture

**Testing a clay soil**

## Clay Soil

To test if your soil is clay-based, roll it into a ball. If the ball stays intact without crumbling, it is clay. Digging clay soils can be backbreaking work: in dry periods clay can bake as hard as a brick, while in wet weather it may be too sticky and heavy to work with. However, clay is also very fertile and easily shares its nutrients. The dense structure of clay means that it doesn't drain very well, so dig in grit, sand, and organic matter to improve its drainage. Plants that prefer heavy soils include Brussels sprouts and broccoli.

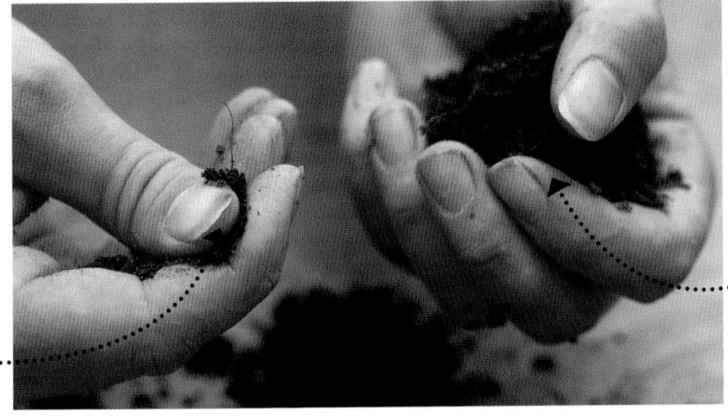

Sandy soils become very loose and crumbly when dry
It is very difficult to form a ball from sandy soil


**Testing a sandy soil**

## Sandy Soil

If the soil crumbles easily between your fingers, it contains a high quantity of sand. Digging in sandy soil is easy. It is light and free-draining, which means that plants are less likely to rot or pick up fungal diseases in wet weather. However, sand is low in nutrients and doesn't retain much moisture, making watering a full-time job in summer. To improve the soil, dig in well-rotted manure or compost and apply fertilizers regularly to supply plants with nutrients. Vegetables that prefer lighter, sandy soils include carrots and parsnips.

## pH testing

Testing to see if your soil is acidic or alkaline is important, since some crops need specific pH levels. Growing a crop in the wrong pH leads to nutrient deficiencies—it can't extract what it needs from the soil. Blueberries, for example, will only thrive in acidic soil so it would be a waste of money to plant them in an alkaline soil that will eventually kill them. If you're unsure of your soil's pH, a simple testing kit can be purchased from a garden center. Soil conditions will only change very gradually, so it is only necessary to test every few years.

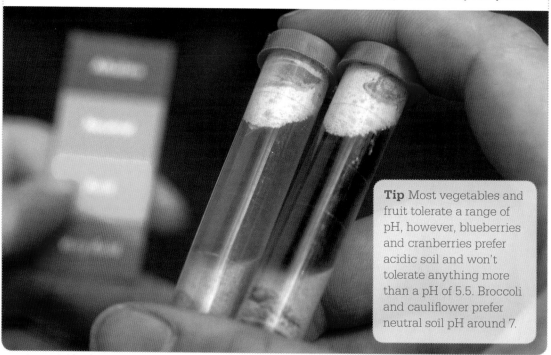

**Tip** Most vegetables and fruit tolerate a range of pH, however, blueberries and cranberries prefer acidic soil and won't tolerate anything more than a pH of 5.5. Broccoli and cauliflower prefer neutral soil pH around 7.

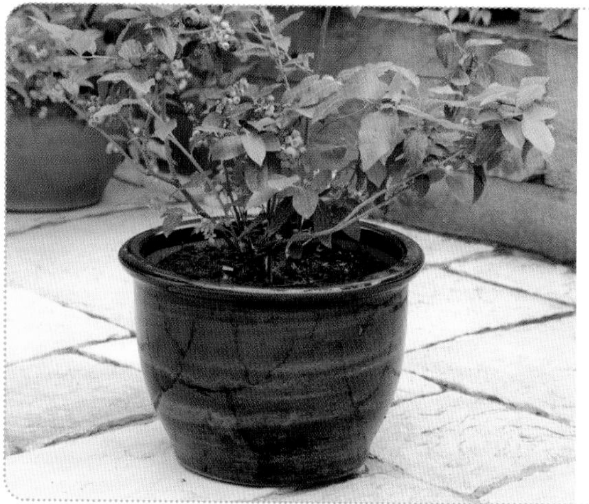

## Controlling conditions

If your soil doesn't suit the crops you want to grow, it is possible to alter the pH. Lime can be added to make conditions more alkaline, and acidic potting mix, sulfur chips, or rotted pine needles can be dug in to make the soil more acidic. However, this will only have a temporary effect on the soil, and these products will eventually wash away. The simplest solution to soils with extreme pH is to grow crops in containers and raised beds. This way you can use an appropriate soil mix and control the conditions more easily.

# Preparing your soil

Before planting, you will need to thoroughly prepare your soil. Put the effort in at this stage, because later it will become difficult to rid the beds of deep-rooted weeds or compacted soil. All your hard work will be well rewarded, since your plants should thrive in these conditions.

**1** If you have recently moved to a new house or are working in a new area in your yard, there may be clutter such as bricks and construction debris littering the ground. Clear it all, and if you need to, use a string trimmer to cut back large swathes of weeds. Dig out any weeds using a fork; a spade will slice through the roots and encourage them to multiply.

*Try to remove weeds in one piece to avoid leaving pieces behind that could regrow*

*Pry deep roots out using your fork*

**2** Once you have cleared all clutter and weeds, the next stage is to thoroughly dig over the soil. Using a spade will help you to dig deeply, breaking up any compaction or large clods of soil below the surface that could impede the roots. Use a fork to lift the soil and sift it. Ideally, try to dig down to twice the depth of the spade or fork.

**3** Once the soil has been dug over, add in some organic matter. The best material to use is homemade garden compost, but you can also buy it from a garden center. Contact your local stables since they may deliver well-rotted manure. After adding the organic matter, the soil should be raked level and left to settle for a few weeks before planting any crops.

*Make sure that compost is well-rotted—otherwise it can scorch crops*

*Use a fork to lightly dig the organic material into the soil*

# Growing locations

Growing your own crops is simple. You don't need an orchard, a community garden plot, or even a huge yard. Most crops can be grown in pots, window boxes, and raised beds, allowing you to grow tasty produce in spaces as small as patios, balconies, and roof gardens. You could even get creative and grow crops in old rain boots, plasticware, or even an old kitchen sink.

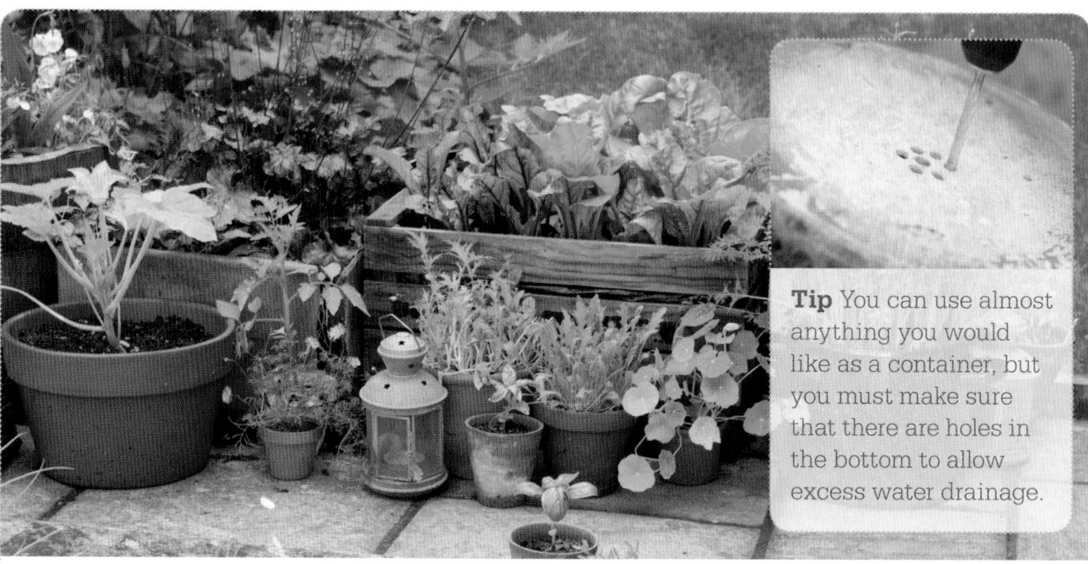

**Tip** You can use almost anything you would like as a container, but you must make sure that there are holes in the bottom to allow excess water drainage.

## Containers

Containers are a great choice for growing crops: they can be moved during the season to ensure sunlight reaches all sides, and weeding is simple since there is hardly any bare soil to cultivate. Choose cold-resistant outdoor pots and consider the size carefully before sowing—some crops such as carrots will need a deeper pot than shallow rooted plants such as lettuce. Since pots drain faster than beds and borders, you will need to remember to water the plants regularly and give them a weekly liquid fertilizer.

## Window boxes

If you want to make the most of your outdoor space and you have a window ledge to spare, consider growing crops in a window box. They are ideal placed outside the kitchen so that you can easily harvest a handful of fresh herbs or salad leaves while you are cooking. Make regular sowings all year long to ensure that there is always something tasty to harvest within reach.

Raised beds

Srawberry boots

## Raised beds

A raised bed is the perfect solution if you have poor-quality soil since you can simply start fresh and fill it with rich new potting mix. The extra height means that the soil will drain well and warm up quickly in spring, and crops will be at a more convenient height to harvest. Raised beds can be made from recycled wood such as railroad ties or pallets, but if you're not confident of your DIY skills, there are plenty of raised-bed kits available.

## Unusual locations

Be imaginative with where you grow your next meal. Recycle materials such as old bowls, juice cartons, and colanders to use as containers. Even old gardening boots can be filled with soil and planted with trailing crops such as strawberries. Larger items such as old wheelbarrows or an old kitchen sink could also make an excellent growing environment—just make sure that whatever you use has drainage holes in the base.

# Choosing a site

Before you get started with sowing or planting, it's worth taking the time to get to know your plot. Figure out which areas are bathed in sunlight and which parts are often in shade. Check this at different times of the day as the sun moves across the sky. Also check to see where the prevailing wind is and identify whether there are any particular areas that are prone to frost.

**Sun-loving squash**

**Shade-loving Swiss chard**

## Sunshine and shade

While crops that are grown in pots can be moved between sunshine and shade to suit, those that are grown in the ground do not have this luxury and must be planted in a suitable location. Most plants prefer full sun—for example, Mediterranean-type plants such as tomatoes, eggplant, peppers, and squash should be planted where they won't be shaded by other plants. However, don't worry if you have a shady site because some plants will tolerate partial or full shade. Leafy crops like Swiss chard and spinach, along with members of the cabbage family, such as Brussels sprouts, broccoli, and cauliflower, will generally tolerate moderate shade. Cooking apples, gooseberries, and red currants will grow on cool, north-facing walls, while rhubarb is ideal for smothering weeds in shady corners of the garden.

## Sheltered sites

Strong winds can knock over tall plants such as sweet corn and shred the leaves of leafy crops. Particularly fierce gusts can also damage fruit trees by causing them to rock in the soil, damaging their roots. If your site is particularly exposed, you may want to create windbreaks to prevent this from happening. The most useful type of protection is a hedge because it deflects the wind but doesn't block it completely. Air movement is important—it prevents the build-up of pests and diseases. Consider using bulky plants such as rows of runner beans or blackberry bushes to protect your more tender crops. Alternatively, plant a mixed hedge from hawthorn, elder, wild roses, and blackthorn, because this is great for wildlife.

## Frost protection

Frost does most of its damage in spring, when young tender crops are planted out and buds and blossoms start to emerge on fruit trees and bushes. There are various methods of protection, but the most common is to cover plants with a cloche or row cover—these are coverings that are placed over crops to keep them warm. Fabric can also be draped over fruit trees or laid over recently sown vegetables. Always listen to the weather forecast and be patient—wait until the risk of frost is over before planting out.

# **The science of** The Life Cycle of Plants

Understanding the key stages in a plant's growth cycle is essential to becoming a good gardener. A plant's main concern is to produce seed so that it can reproduce. Seed is dispersed by various methods including wind, animals, water, or of course, by gardeners.

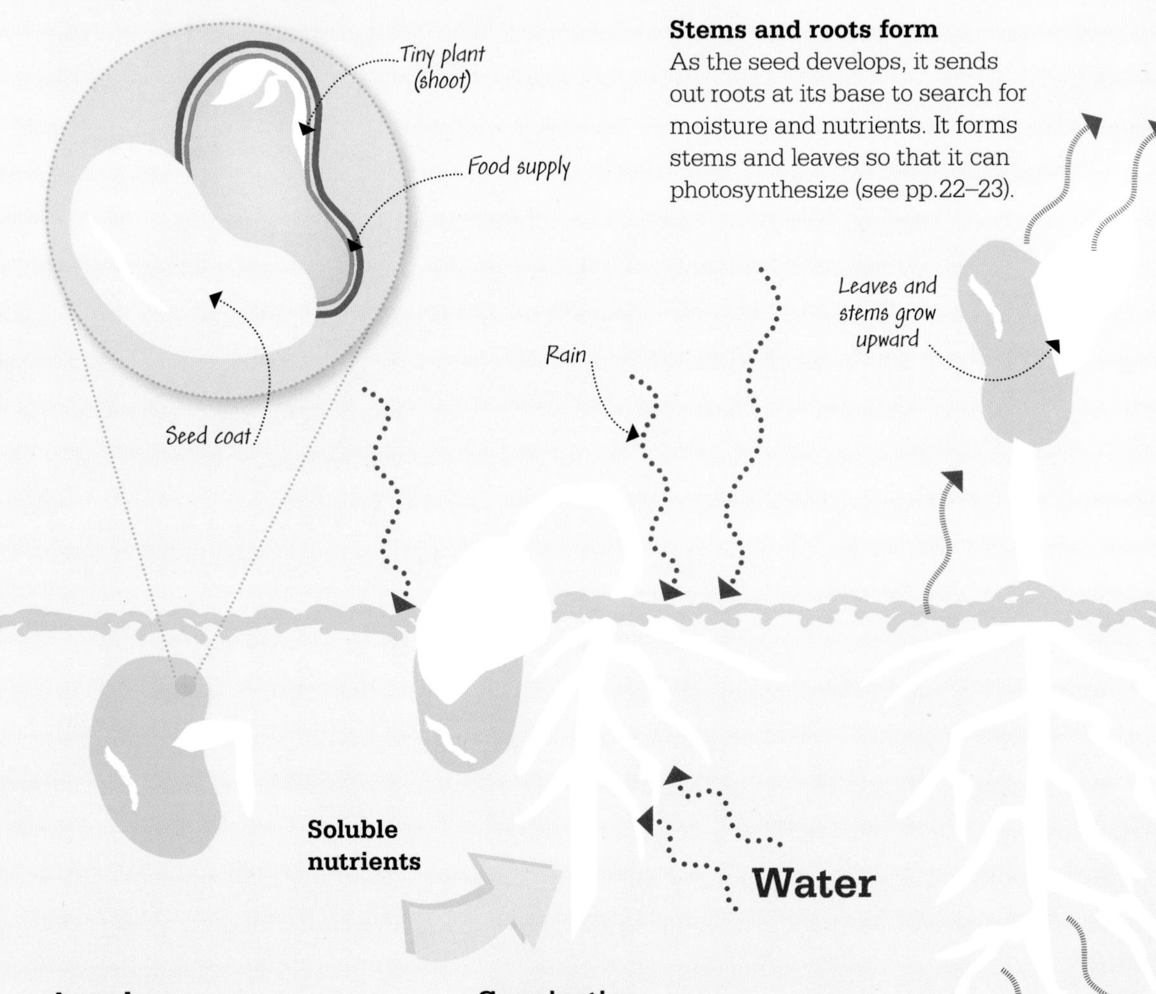


### Stems and roots form

As the seed develops, it sends out roots at its base to search for moisture and nutrients. It forms stems and leaves so that it can photosynthesize (see pp.22–23).

### A seed

This is the first and last stage of a plant's life. Although it may look lifeless, it is in fact a plant resting in its early embryonic stages before it bursts into life.

### Germination

This is the first stage in the seed's development and is prompted by adequate warmth, moisture, and soil. The first sign of life is a shoot breaking through the seed coat.

Sun

Light energy

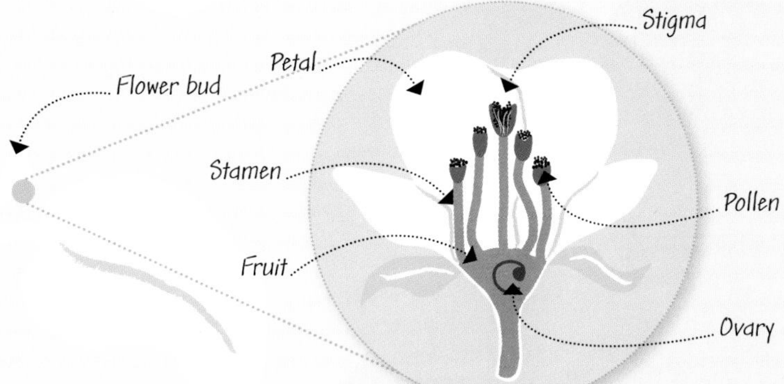


Carbon dioxide

**Flowers form**
To produce fruit and seeds, flowers must be fertilized by pollinating insects. The more colorful and scented the flower, the more insects it will attract.

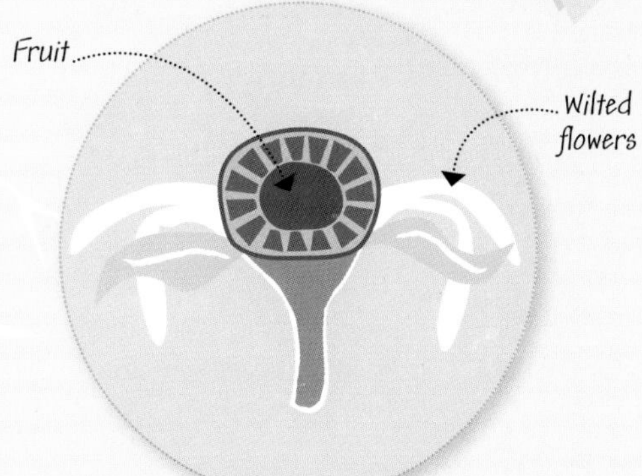


Roots continue to branch out and down

**Fruit develops**
Pollination occurs when pollen is transferred from a male stamen onto a female stigma. The ovary swells to become the seed-filled fruit.

# **The science of** Photosynthesis

This is the necessary process by which plants create their food and energy. Without this they wouldn't be able to grow. The key raw ingredients are light, water, and carbon dioxide, which are converted into sugar and oxygen. Carbon dioxide is received from the air through their leaves, light is received via the sun, while water is obtained through their roots.

**Sun**

**Light energy**

**Carbon dioxide + Water**

**Light**

**Sugar + Oxygen**

### The movement of carbon dioxide

Plants take in carbon dioxide from the air. The carbon dioxide diffuses into the leaves through tiny holes in the underside of the leaf called stomata (see below, right).

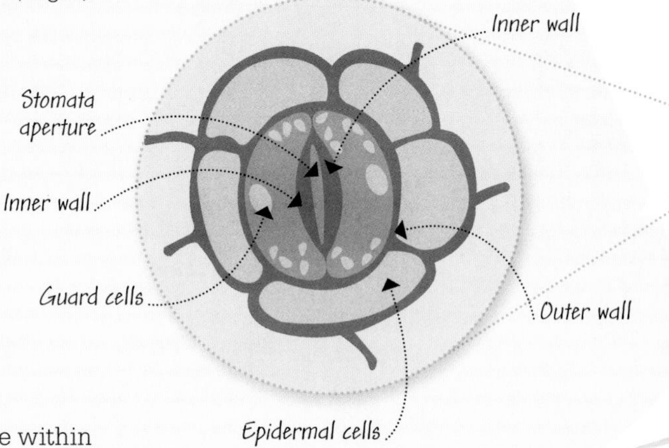


### Leaf structure

Photosynthesis takes place within the plant's cells in structures called chloroplasts. These contain chlorophyll, the green pigment that gives the leaves and stems their color.

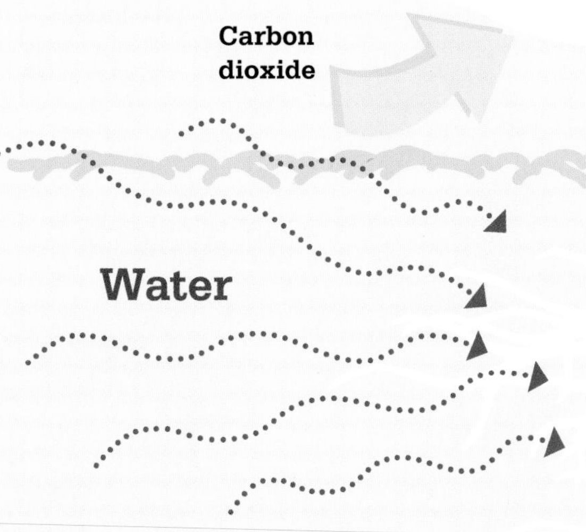


### The movement of water

Plants get the water they need for photosynthesis by absorbing it through their roots. It is drawn up the plant and into the leaves through tubes in the stem known as xylems.

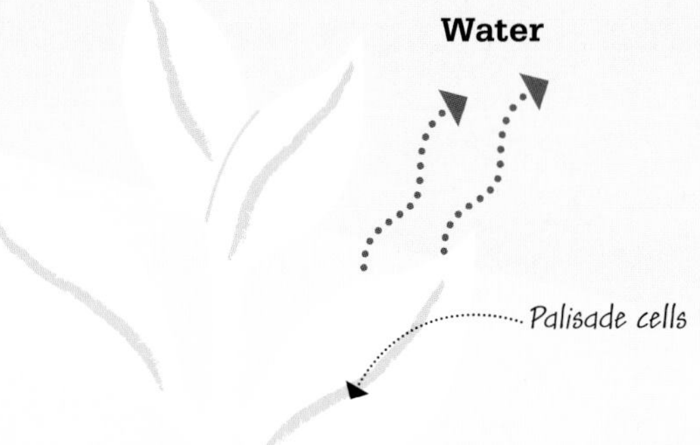


### The role of the sun

Leaves absorb sunlight on the upper part of the leaf via a type of cell called a palisade. This area contains lots of chloroplasts, which absorb the light necessary for photosynthesis to take place.

### The release of oxygen

Plants absorb carbon dioxide from the air, but they also produce and release oxygen. This exchange of gases takes place in stomata found on the underside of the leaf.

### Root structure

Roots are perfectly adapted to allow the plant to absorb water easily—they have a very large surface area and thin cell walls. Water enters through the root hair cells.

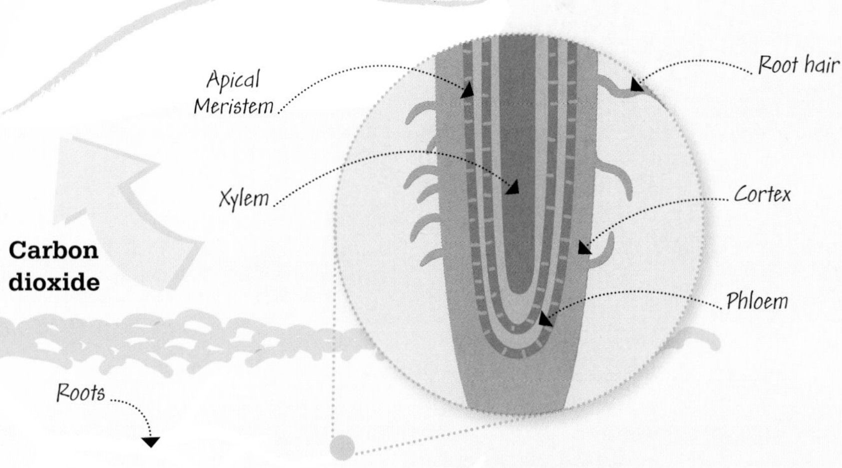


### Sugar storage

The plant converts carbon dioxide and water into oxygen and glucose. This sugar is either used by the plant or converted into long-lasting sugars and stored.

# **The science of** Plant Needs

Plants won't grow properly if they don't get the right nutrients. Most nutrients are taken up from the soil, so you can give your plant a boost by adding fertilizers and soil improvers to your beds. Others reach the plant via the air and water, which is why it's so important to keep plants well watered.

**Sun**

**Structural nutrients**
Carbon, hydrogen, and oxygen are found in the air and water. They are known as structural nutrients since they help to build cellulose, which keeps plants strong and upright. They also contribute to the photosynthesis process.

*Sunlight is absorbed by chlorophyll*

**Primary macronutrients**
The three essential nutrients a plant needs are nitrogen, phosphorus, and potassium. They are found in the soil and are abbreviated to NPK when referred to in fertilizer.

**Secondary macronutrients**
Sulfur, calcium, and magnesium are the next most important elements. Soils are not often lacking in these nutrients, and levels of calcium and magnesium are increased when lime is applied.

*Gases enter the leaves through stomata on the underside*

**Carbon dioxide**

**Micronutrients**
These nutrients are only needed in tiny amounts. They include elements such as boron, copper, manganese, iron, and zinc.

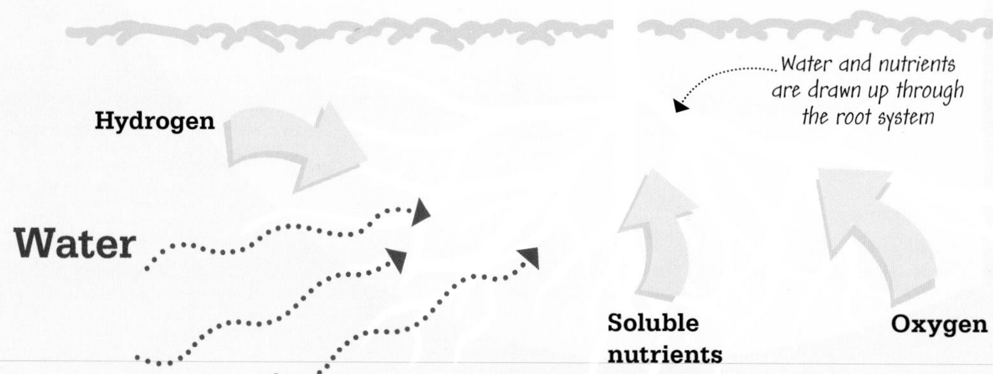

| **Nutrient** | *What it does* | *What happens if the plant doesn't have enough* | *Where it comes from* |
|---|---|---|---|
| Carbon | In photosynthesis it becomes converted to sugar in the plant | The plant won't be able to produce energy for itself and dies | It is taken from carbon dioxide from the surrounding air |
| Hydrogen | Needed for building up sugars during photosynthesis | The lack of hydrogen results in lack of sugar and the plant dies | It is obtained from the air or from water |
| Oxygen | Is needed for the plant to convert the sugar it has made into energy | It would be unlikely for a plant to be depleted of oxygen | It comes from the surrounding air and from water |
| Nitrogen | Helps the plant to produce green, lush growth and foliage | Plant growth stops and the leaves turn yellow, starting at the bottom | The soil and fertilizers; beans and peas absorb it from the atmosphere |
| Phosphorus | It stimulates healthy root growth and rapid growth in plants | Roots don't develop and foliage turns purplish, starting at the bottom | The soil, but also found in fertilizers, such as blood, fish, and bone |
| Potassium | Promotes color, flavor, and resistance to disease | Yellowing and sometimes spotting on the lower leaves | It is found in the soil and often added to fertilizers |
| Sulfur | Promotes chlorophyll formation, root growth, vigor, and hardiness | The plant develops yellow leaves and spindly growth | In the soil, usually from rainwater, also in many fertilizers |
| Calcium | Forms part of the plant cell wall structure and strengthens the plant | Yellowing at the most active sections of plant, such as the leaf tips | In the soil, but also from lime, gypsum, and super-sulfate |
| Magnesium | Forms chlorophyll and is needed for photosynthesis | The leaves start to turn yellow between the veins | In the soil and from organic material, fertilizers, and lime |
| Iron | Key in the development of chlorophyll and the photosynthesis process | Deficiency causes a yellowing around the edge of the foliage | Found in the soil but also common in fertilizers |
| Zinc | Helps to control and regulate the consumption of sugars | A deficiency causes malformed leaves or fruit | Found in the soil but is also common in fertilizers |
| Manganese | It assists in the breakdown of sugars for the plant | The leaves start to turn yellow between the veins | It is commonly found in the soil |
| Copper | Aids growth and helps with the metabolism of sugars | The plant develops yellowing in the upper leaves | Found in the soil and in fertilizers |

# 1

# Start Simple

Growing your own fruit and vegetables is an incredibly rewarding experience. Once you've mastered the basics and learned how to give plants the care they need, there's a large number of crops to choose from, even if you only have a small garden. This chapter starts you off with some of the easiest and most reliable crops, from fresh leafy salads to sweet and juicy strawberries.

## In this section learn to grow:

**Salad greens**
*see pp.36–39*

**Tomatoes**
*see pp.42–45*

**Herbs**
*see pp.48–51*

**Onions**
*see pp.52–55*

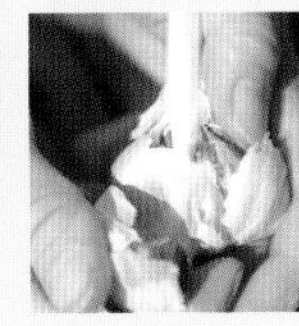

**Garlic**
*see pp.56–59*

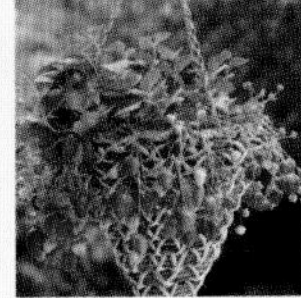

**Strawberries**
*see pp.60–64*

# How to **Sow Seeds**

Seeing the young shoots of crops you've sown is always exciting. Seeds can be bought from your local garden center or online, or simply collected from plants grown the previous year. Some crops can be sown directly outdoors, others will need to be started off indoors.

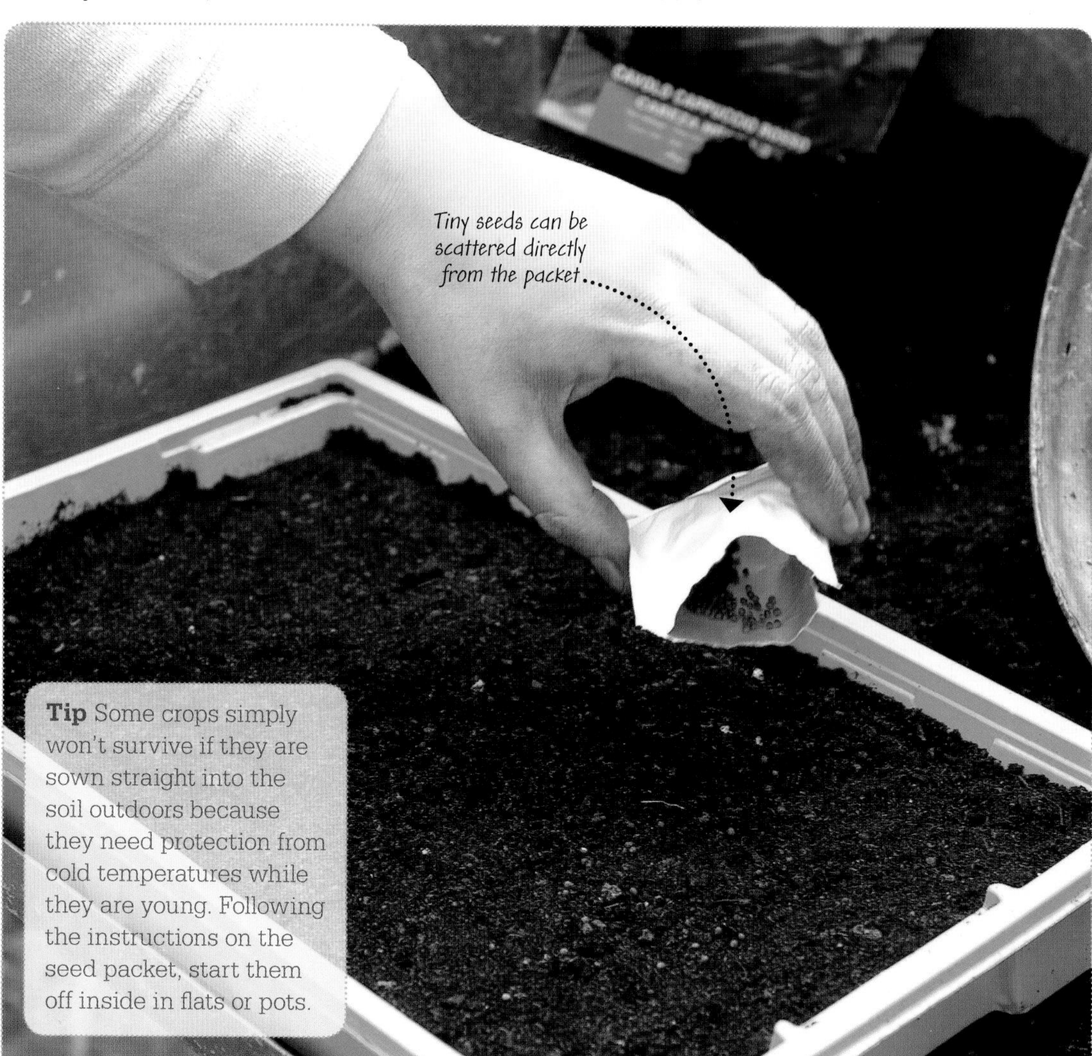

Tiny seeds can be scattered directly from the packet


**Tip** Some crops simply won't survive if they are sown straight into the soil outdoors because they need protection from cold temperatures while they are young. Following the instructions on the seed packet, start them off inside in flats or pots.

## Sowing in flats

For tiny seeds, such as lettuce, fill a seed flat with propagation mix and lightly firm down. Scatter the seeds over the surface, then lightly cover them with more mix. Water and cover the flat with glass or a clear plastic lid and keep in a warm, light place, such as on a windowsill, to allow the seeds to germinate. Remove the cover as soon as shoots appear.

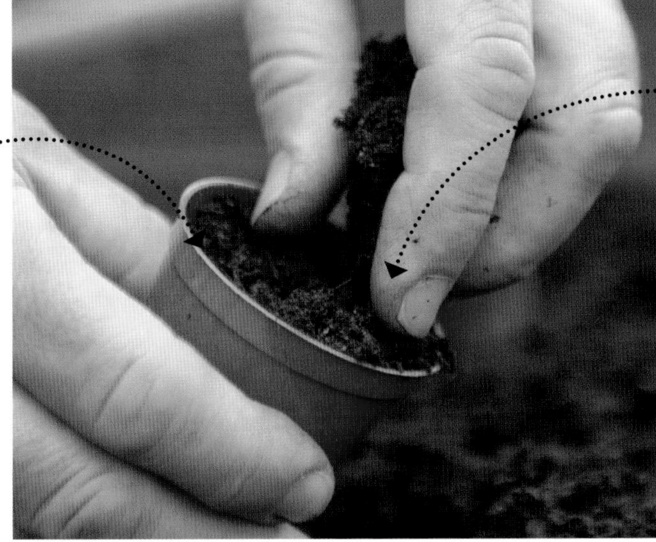

Press down the potting mix with your fingers or the base of another pot
Always use a high quality potting mix to produce healthy plants


**Fill the pot with potting mix**

Remember to water seeds after sowing
Use your finger to gently cover the seed with mix


**Cover the seed with potting mix**

## Sowing in pots

Larger seeds, such as runner beans, can be sown into individual pots. Fill the pots with general-purpose potting mix and make a hole using a dibber or your finger. Drop one seed into each hole and cover with more mix. Always water the seeds after sowing. Cover each pot with a plastic bag, secured with a rubberband, until the first shoots appear.

# How to **Plant Out**

Whether you have grown your own plants from seeds or bought them from the garden center, timing is everything when it comes to planting them outdoors. Plant them out too early and they may get frost-damaged; too late and they could become pot bound and unhealthy.

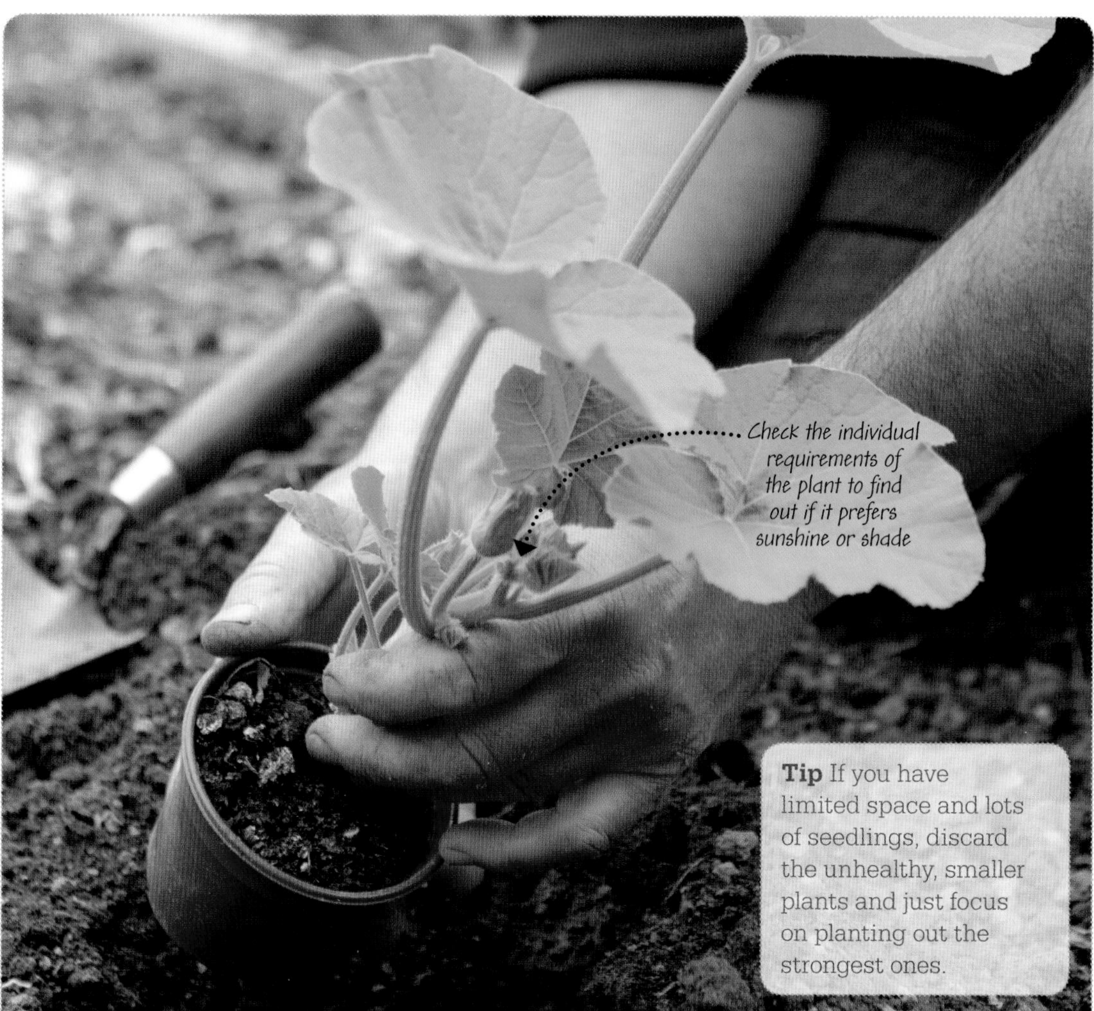

*Check the individual requirements of the plant to find out if it prefers sunshine or shade*

**Tip** If you have limited space and lots of seedlings, discard the unhealthy, smaller plants and just focus on planting out the strongest ones.

## Taking a plant out of its pot

Gently remove the plant from its pot by lightly squeezing the base with one hand, taking care not to damage the roots. Use your other hand to hold the plant carefully by the base of the stem, making sure that it doesn't bend or break. For seeds grown in flats, hold the seedling gently by its leaves and tease out its fragile roots with a dibber or blunt pencil.

Prepare the soil thoroughly before planting by digging it over, removing any weeds, and adding well-rotted manure or compost

Push the plant in firmly to ensure the roots are in contact with the soil

## Planting in the ground

Dig a hole the same depth as the pot and line the base with soil mix. Be careful not to plant too deeply, or the stem will start to rot. However, if not planted deep enough, the root ball will quickly dry out and start to wilt. Firm the plant into the soil with your fingertips after planting.

Avoid getting water on the leaves—this can scorch them if they get a lot of sunshine

Always give plants a big drink after planting them outside

## Watering in

Use a fine nozzle on your watering can to sprinkle water gently around your new plant —this way you can give it a thorough soaking without risking damage to its leaves or stem. Watering the plant in well will help the roots settle into the new soil.

# How to **Water Your Plants**

Water is vital to keep your plants alive and healthy, so it is essential that you do not let them dry out. However, it is also important to try to conserve water in the yard. Use rain barrels to collect rainwater and water the plants in the morning or evening when the temperature is coolest so that the plants can absorb the water before it evaporates.

A nozzle on the end of a watering can distributes the water equally and gently around the plants
Try to avoid watering the leaves—instead, water around the root system
Ensure that the container has adequate drainage holes


## Watering cans

There are many methods for watering plants. A watering can is ideal if you have a small yard or several pots close to your house. It is a little more work if your garden is a long way from the tap or rain barrel, but may be the only way if water restrictions are in place.

Aim the hose toward the base of the plants, to avoid damaging them

This attachment has a long handle, making it easy to reach faraway plants

## Garden hoses

Using a hose is an easy and efficient way to water your plants. Many garden hoses have attachment heads with a range of different settings, which allow you to accurately control the placement and amount of water you are giving to your plants.

Water seeps directly into the soil through holes in a hose

Regular watering will keep your plants green and healthy

## Soaker hoses

Soaker hoses have tiny perforations in the piping through which a regular or controlled supply of water goes directly to your plants' roots, where it is most needed. Laid on the ground, these hoses keep the soil moist, encouraging your garden to grow.

# How to **Tie In and Pinch Off**

Some crops have a natural tendency to use their energy to grow large and leafy rather than produce plump fruit and vegetables, but there are ways to control this. Rampant growth can be kept under control by tying in the plants, keeping them neat and easy to manage. At other times, plants may need their shoots pinched off to redirect their growth.

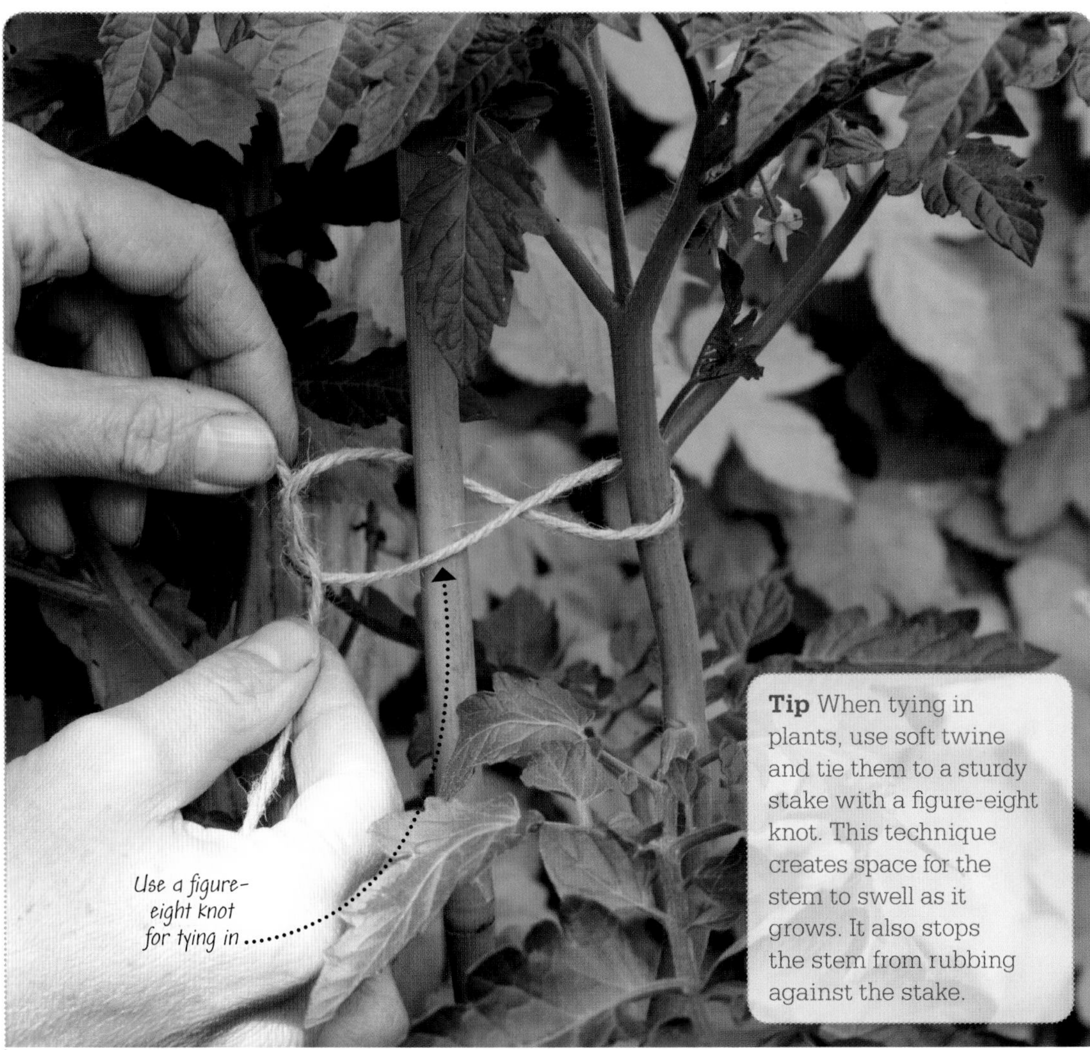
Use a figure-eight knot for tying in

**Tip** When tying in plants, use soft twine and tie them to a sturdy stake with a figure-eight knot. This technique creates space for the stem to swell as it grows. It also stops the stem from rubbing against the stake.

## Tying in

Plants such as tomatoes, eggplants, and peppers need to be regularly tied in since they grow quickly through the summer months. Use a sturdy stake to keep them upright and in place. Remember, too, that as their fruit grows heavier they will need a lot of support.

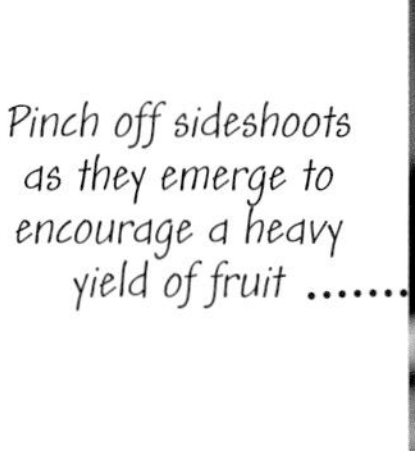

Pinch off sideshoots as they emerge to encourage a heavy yield of fruit

**Pinching off sideshoots**

Pinching off the growing tips will create a bushy plant
Pinch the tip of the plant back to a lower set of leaves


**Pinching off the growing tips**

## Pinching off

There are two reasons for pinching back a plant. Pinching off sideshoots on plants such as tomatoes ensures that their energy goes into producing fruit rather than leaves. And pinching off the growing tips of leaf crops, such as basil, encourages bushier growth.

# Grow Salad in a Window Box

Growing salad in a window box is easy and produces quick, delicious results—it will also be much cheaper than buying bags of supermarket salad. Because the leaves are close at hand, it is easy to keep an eye on them to make sure they don't dry out, and they are ideally placed for harvesting.

full sun or part shade

moist soil

## Equipment

Window box
Crocks or mesh screening
General-purpose potting mix
Trowel
Bamboo pole
Packet of seeds
  such as lettuce, arugula, or spinach
Watering can with a fine nozzle
Scissors

Window box

General-purpose potting mix

Bamboo poles

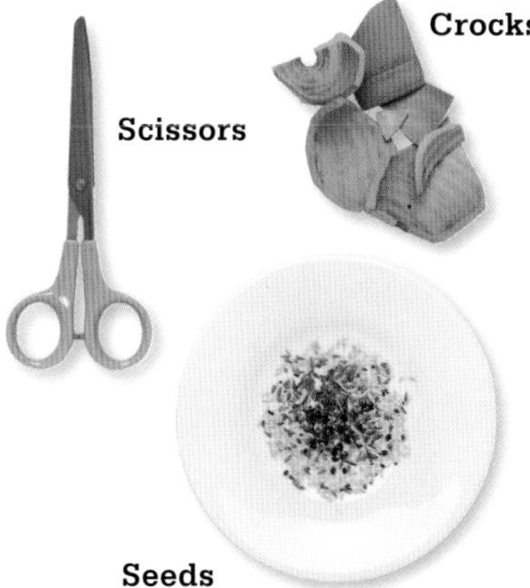
Scissors

Crocks

Seeds

Watering can

Trowel

**Salad leaves** *4–6 weeks until harvest*

**Sow** *all year indoors; mid-spring to early fall outside*

**Water** *the seedlings well, especially in hot summer weather*

**Harvest** *all year indoors; mid-spring to mid-fall outside*

**1** Place some crocks or mesh screening over the drainage holes in the bottom of the window box, then fill it up with high-quality, all-purpose potting mix. Water the surface lightly using a watering can with a fine nozzle, then push a piece of bamboo cane lengthwise into the mix to create shallow furrows.

**Tip** Germination will be quicker if the soil is slightly damp.

Use a pencil if you do not have a piece of bamboo

Leave a gap of about ½in (1cm) from the top of the window box

Sprinkle the seeds using your thumb and forefinger

**2** Tip the seeds into the palm of your hand and sprinkle them into the soil at the spacing recommended on the seed packet.

**Tip** If the seeds are tiny, mix them with some sand—this will allow you to see where you have sown, so that you don't miss any furrows or accidentally sow twice.

*Be careful not to brush the seeds out of their furrows*

**3** Lightly cover the seeds with soil mix and place on a sunny or partly shaded windowsill. Water the plants regularly to keep the soil moist. In four to six weeks, once the leaves are ready to harvest, cut them just above the base every few days so that they can resprout.

**Careful!** The plants may need watering every day in summer—window boxes dry out quickly.

## Caring for your **Salad Leaves**

Salad leaves are very easy to grow, but you will need to water them regularly and protect them from slugs to guarantee the very best crop.

*Cut leaves while they're still young and fresh*

*After harvesting, a new crop of leaves will grow back in a couple of weeks*

### Things to watch out for...

**Wilted leaves** Window boxes drain quickly, especially when they are in a sunny location, so if your leaves are looking limp or wilted, they will need a thorough soaking. Water them well, and regularly check the surface of the soil to make sure it hasn't dried out. Nourish the plants with a liquid fertilizer once a week to prevent them from running out of energy.

**Slugs and snails** These common garden pests can devour your salad crops, which may not be completely safe even in a window box. Regularly check the plants for signs of damage and see pp.66–67 for tips on how to deal with them. Caterpillars may also attack your plants; remove them by hand as soon as you spot them.

**Garden thieves** If birds are a problem, you may need to protect crops with a net.

**Also learn to grow ▸▸▸**

# How to grow **Lettuce and Edible flowers**

**full sun or part shade**

**moist soil**

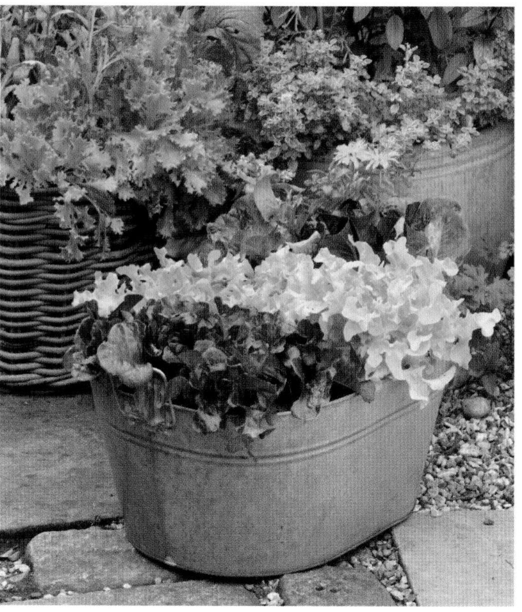
**Lettuce**

## Equipment

- Lettuce or edible flower seeds
- A container such as a window box
- General-purpose potting mix
- Watering can

Tender salad leaves and edible flowers, such as nasturtiums, calendula, and violas, can be grown easily in containers, and are shallow-rooted so are ideal for window boxes. They are so quick to grow that within weeks of planting you'll be picking delicious flower heads or succulent leaves that will add color and flavor to your salads.

### SOWING

**Sow the seeds in spring** in containers filled with general-purpose potting mix. Make shallow furrows and sprinkle the seeds in carefully. Cover them with potting mix and water in well. Once the seedlings start to show, ensure they get plenty of sunlight. Water them regularly, remembering to water the soil surface and not the tender leaves.

**Thin out the seedlings** if they become crowded. When thinning lettuce seedlings, don't discard them; wash and add to salads as baby leaves.

**Edible flowers**

### HARVESTING

**Lettuce should be fully grown** in around 10–12 weeks, and can be harvested whole. Alternatively, harvest leaves as tasty cut-and-come-again crops.

**Edible flowers will be ready** to harvest in about 5–6 weeks. Pick the blooming flower heads regularly and lay them out on paper towels so any insects can be easily removed. Avoid washing them if you can, and store in a plastic bag in the refrigerator for a couple of hours before using.

# How to grow **Spinach and Swiss Chard**

full sun or part shade

moist soil

## Equipment

- Spinach or Swiss chard seeds
- A container such as a window box
- General-purpose potting mix
- Watering can

Once you have tasted homegrown spinach and Swiss chard leaves, you will want your own supply of them all year round. These crops are very easy to grow as well as being highly nutritious.

### SOWING

**Sow the seeds** in shallow furrows. Cover them with potting mix and water in well. In a few weeks when the seedlings are large enough to handle, thin them out. Don't discard the thinnings—wash them and use in salads as baby leaves. To ensure bumper crops, make sure you keep the plants well watered and nourished because the shallow containers will dry out very quickly.

### HARVESTING

**In window boxes,** both spinach and Swiss chard plants should be picked while the leaves are still small, within about six weeks. Harvest the baby leaves and use them in salads. If the leaves of your plants have grown slightly larger, try stir-frying them, which will preserve their nutrients.

### TROUBLESHOOTING

**Spinach is prone to bolting,** which is when the plant rushes to flower and produce seed, making the leaves unusable. This usually occurs if the soil mix has been allowed to dry out, so it is important to keep it moist at all times. Water the plants once—or even twice—a day if necessary during warm, dry weather.

**Spinach**

**Swiss chard**

# Grow Tomatoes in a Pot

Harvesting a bumper crop of juicy, homegrown tomatoes warmed by the summer sun is really satisfying. Growing this versatile vegetable can be as simple as planting and caring for a store-bought plant, so grab some from the garden center and grow a supply of tomatoes all summer.

full sun

moist soil

## Equipment

- Tomato plant
- Terra-cotta container
- Crocks
- Peat-free potting mix
- Trowel
- Bamboo poles
- String
- Scissors
- Watering can
- Liquid tomato fertilizer

**Tomato plant**

**String**

**Terra-cotta pot**

**Peat-free potting mix**

**Liquid tomato fertilizer**

**Watering can**

**Scissors**

**Crocks**

**Trowel**

**Bamboo poles**

**Tomatoes** *8–16 weeks until harvest*

**Plant** *out between late spring and early summer*

**Water daily** *and feed every two weeks once fruit appears*

**Harvest** *in midsummer to mid-fall*

**1** Tomato plants are ideal for growing in containers in a sunny, sheltered location. Water the plant a couple of hours before planting, then gently remove it from its pot, being careful not to damage the roots. Partially fill your new container with general-purpose potting mix.

**Careful!** If you are growing the tomato as an upright, or "cordon" plant, avoid trailing varieties.

*Be careful when handling the plant to ensure the stem does not snap*

*Leave a small gap between the soil mix surface and the top of the pot*

**2** Place the tomato plant into the container, and fill around the root ball with potting mix, making sure that the base of the stem is flush with the level of the mix in the container. Gently firm the tomato plant into the soil mix, using your fingertips.

**3** Once the tomato plant is in place, it will need to be supported, since once the fruit develops it will become top-heavy—a bamboo pole is the simplest method (see p.77). Push the stake into the soil, making sure that you don't drive it through the plant's root system, and tie the plant to it with twine. Water the plant daily and give it tomato fertilizer once a week.

*Leave a 4-in (10-cm) gap between the plant and the stake*

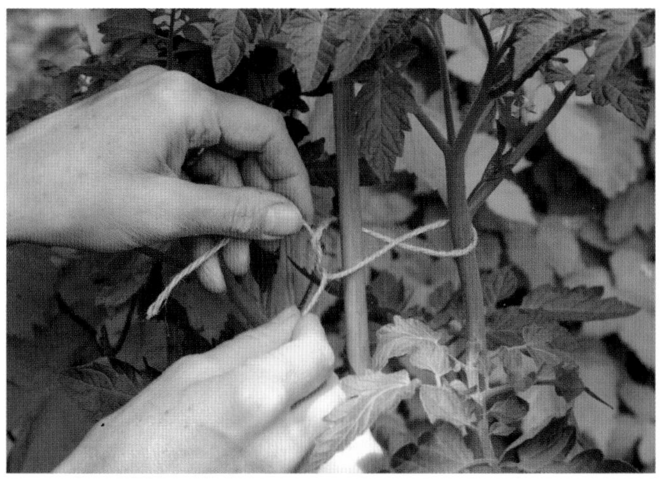

**4** The tomato plant will need to be tied in regularly as it grows, using a figure-eight knot to avoid damaging the stem (see p.34). Encourage fruiting by pinching off sideshoots growing from the leaf joints (see p.35). Pick the tomatoes when they turn red and are slightly soft.

**Tip** Toward the end of the season they can be picked green and left to ripen on a windowsill.

## Caring for your **Tomatoes**

Tomatoes are the quintessential Mediterranean fruit and thrive in sunny spots, but will need regular watering to prevent them from drying out.

### Things to watch out for...

**Whiteflies** These pests can swarm a plant, sucking sap from the underside of the leaves and causing mold to form. If they become a serious problem, you may want to consider using insecticide. Plant marigolds near the tomatoes and they may help to ward off whiteflies.

**Potassium deficiency** If the leaves turn brown and blotchy and there aren't many tomatoes on your plant, it may be short of potassium. Feed the plants once a week with a tomato fertilizer that is high in potassium, which gives the tomatoes flavor and color. Keep plants well watered to boost their general level of health (see p.66).

**Tomato blight** If the leaves, stems, and tomatoes start to look brown and diseased, and then begin to rot, remove the plant immediately and destroy it.

*Don't forget to support the cordon with a stake, otherwise it will snap*

*Pick tomatoes when slightly soft and allow them to ripen fully indoors*

**Also learn to grow ▸▸▸**

# How to grow **Herbs in a Pot**

full sun

light soil

## Equipment

Chive or basil plants

Pot of any size or shape, with drainage holes

Mesh screening or crocks

Good-quality potting mix

Watering can

As well as being an attractive addition to the garden, chives and basil are delicious ingredients for use in a variety of dishes. Keep the plants well watered, and give them a sheltered, sunny site.

### PLANTING

**Before you plant the herbs** in their new container, water them thoroughly an hour before planting. Turn over each pot and ease out the plant. If the plant is large and you want to divide it, hold the plant at its base, gently pry apart the root ball, and separate the plant into smaller clumps.

**Place screening** or crocks in the base of your new container and then cover with a layer of high-quality potting mix. Arrange your herb plants in the pot in a design, making sure that there is even coverage and that there are plants around its edge. Leave about 4in (10cm) between plants. Fill in the gaps in the soil mix and firm around the plants. Leave a gap of 1in (2.5cm) between the top of the soil mix and the pot's rim. Water well and place the pot in a sunny spot.

**Tip** This method can be used with any number of herb plants, so feel free to experiment depending on the herbs you like to use.

**Chives**

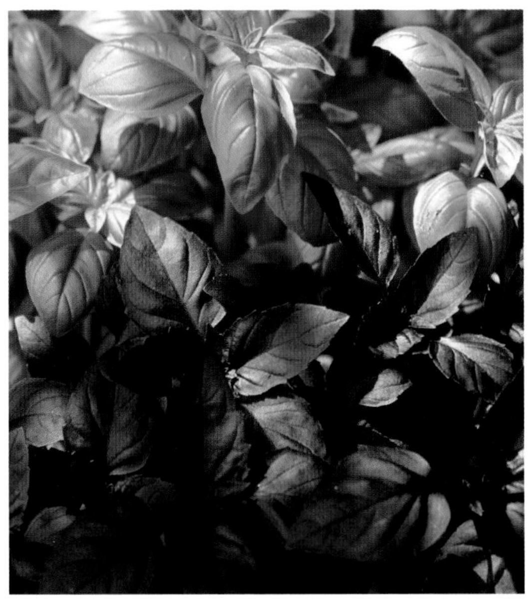

**Basil**

# How to grow **Roots in a Pot**

full sun

light soil

**Radishes**

## Equipment

- Radish or beet seeds
- Pot of any size or shape, with drainage holes
- Mesh screening or crocks
- High-quality potting mix
- Watering can

Radishes and baby beets are ideal crops to grow for quick results. You will be picking these nutritious and tasty roots about 4–5 weeks after sowing. As soon as one crop is done, sow another.

### SOWING

**Fill your pot with potting mix** to within 1in (2.5cm) of the rim and water well. Scatter the seeds lightly on the surface and cover with more mix. Water the seeds in well. Put the pot in a sunny site and remember to keep it well watered.

### GROWING

**When the seedlings** appear, you may need to thin them to give them space to swell in size. Beet seedlings need to be about 2in (5cm) apart, and radishes 1in (2.5cm). Don't throw away any seedlings, instead wash and add to salads.

### HARVESTING

**Begin harvesting** as soon as your crops reach an edible size. After about 4–5 weeks your baby beets and your radishes should be 1in (2.5cm) in size; don't leave them in the pot for too long, or they will turn dry and pithy. Remember to harvest baby beet leaves as well as their roots.

**Tip** Radishes will tolerate shade and can be planted between taller plants, such as lettuce.

**Baby beets**

# Grow Herbs in a Basket

Create a basket of aromas just outside your kitchen window with this beautiful display of herbs. Easy to grow no matter how small your space, this selection of herbs can be adapted to suit your culinary tastes.

full sun

light soil

## Equipment

- Hanging basket with plastic liner
- General-purpose potting mix
- Horticultural grit
- Herb plants
  such as rosemary, chives, sage, marjoram, thyme, and lemon verbena
- Trowel
- Watering can
- Wall bracket
- Drill and screws

**Hanging basket**

**General-purpose potting mix**

**Horticultural grit**

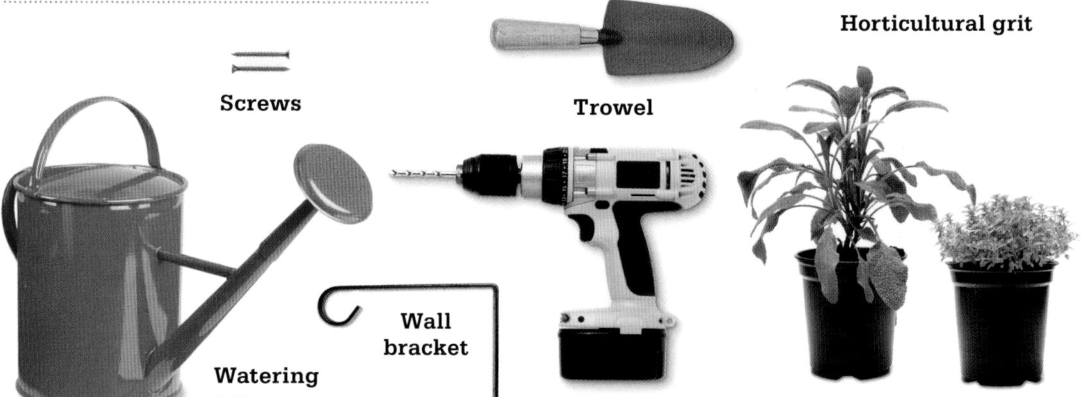

**Screws**

**Trowel**

**Watering can**

**Wall bracket**

**Drill**

**Herb plants**

**Herbs** *4–16 weeks until harvest*

**Plant out** *your herbs between mid-spring and midsummer*

**Water** *young plants well, especially in hot summer weather*

**Harvest** *crops all year round, as you require them*

**1** If the basket is not lined, line it with a basket liner or plastic sheeting. Herbs grow best in well-drained conditions, so mix general-purpose potting mix with grit at a ratio of 5:1 and place this in the bottom of the basket.

**Careful!** Make sure the liner has drainage holes. If not, pierce it with a knife or scissors.

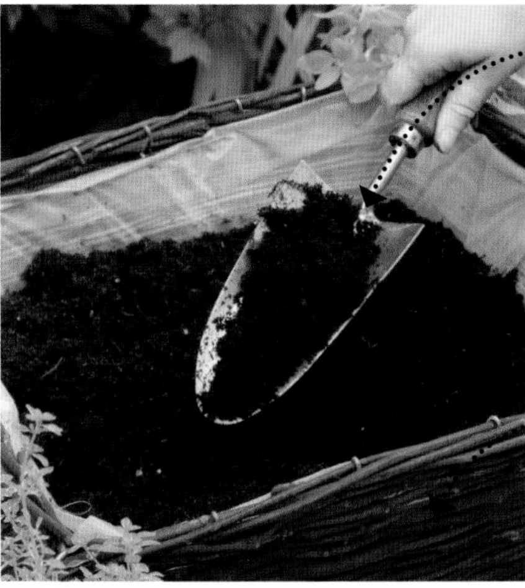

Fill the container halfway, leaving enough space for the plants

Choose an attractive container if it is to hang in a prominent position

Some herbs can be split if they are too big

**2** Choose plants that you enjoy using while cooking. Plant the more upright herbs in the center with the trailing varieties on the outside. You could also use annual flowers with trailing habits.

**Tip** Avoid mint; it is invasive and will swamp other plants.

**3** There should be room for about five to six plants in an average-sized hanging basket. Place the herbs in the basket, and pack the soil mix and grit around the root balls, firming in with your fingertips.

**Tip** Only fill the basket up to 1in (2.5cm) below the basket rim, to allow space for it to be watered without overflowing.

Reach in between the plants to ensure they are all firmed in well

**4** Water the herbs thoroughly after planting. Hang the basket from a sturdy bracket in a warm, sheltered site. Water the plants at least once a day during summer and give them liquid fertilizer each week. In winter, only water if the soil is very dry.

**Tip** Water in the morning or evening when the temperature is coolest so plants can absorb water before it evaporates.

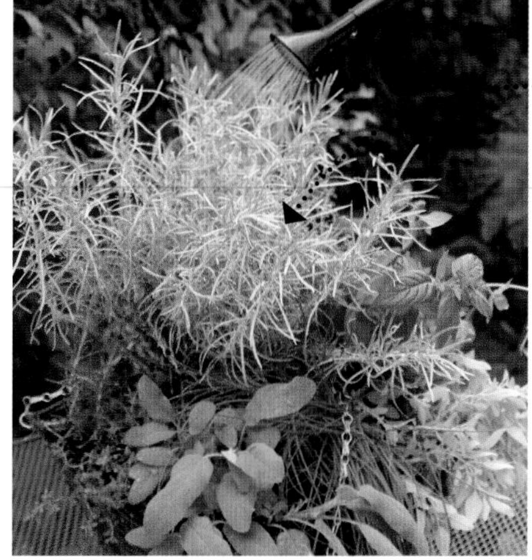

*Use a fine nozzle at the end of the watering can to gently distribute the water*

# Caring for your **Herbs**

Hanging baskets filled with herbs make the best use of a small growing space, and will only need some simple care to keep the plants healthy and happy.

## Things to watch out for...

**Wilted leaves** Hanging baskets filled with free-draining soil will dry out very quickly, and you may find that you need to water the plants most days during the summer. Check the drainage holes so that the herbs don't sit in overly damp conditions.

**Powdery coating on leaves and stems** Mildew creates a whitish layer on the herb foliage and may cause the leaves to become distorted in shape. Remove all infected plant material and ensure that the plants are getting enough sunshine, that their soil is not overly damp, and thin out some of the plants so that there is a good airflow around them.

**New growth** Regularly harvest the leaves and shoots to encourage new growth. Some herbs, such as rosemary, will benefit from a light trim in spring.

**Cramped conditions** The herbs in this selection are perennial and can keep going for a few years. However, because of the restricted growing conditions, some of them will benefit from being divided in the fall and potted into a new hanging basket with fresh potting mix and grit.

*For a vibrant display, choose herbs that provide a contrast of colors and textures*

# Grow Onions from Sets

If you love cooking, onions are surely a must for your kitchen garden. Although they can be grown from seed, it is far easier to plant onion sets, which are basically mini-onions and can be planted straight into the ground in fall or spring.

full sun

light soil

## Equipment

- Onion sets
- Fork
- Rake
- Bamboo poles
- Twine
- Watering can
- Hoe
- Plant labels
- General-purpose fertilizer

Onion sets

Twine

General-purpose fertilizer

Fork

Hoe

Bamboo poles

Plant labels

Watering can

Rake

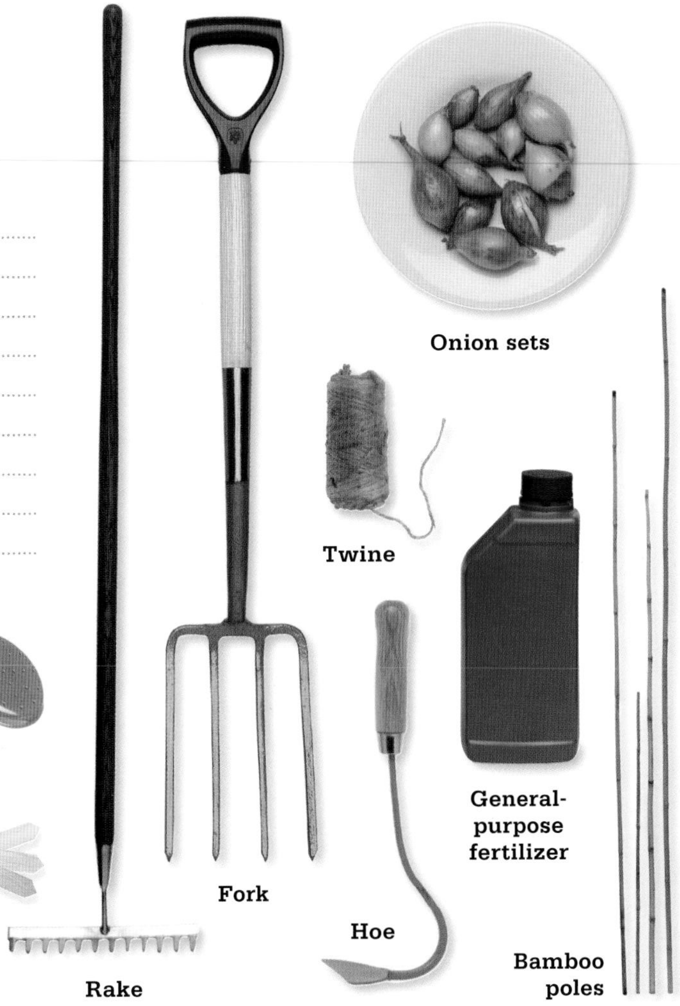

**Onions** *20–24 weeks until harvest*

**Plant out sets** *in fall or early to mid-spring*

**Weed** *carefully around the seedlings as they develop*

**Harvest** *onions between early summer and mid-fall*

**1** In a sunny location, mark out furrows 12in (30cm) apart with string (see p.72). Create a ridge in the soil using a hoe and push the onion sets into the soil, leaving just the tip of each one showing above the soil. Space them 3–4in (8–10cm) apart.

**Careful!** Avoid planting the sets into freshly manured soil—this can cause them to rot.

*Be careful not to damage your young plants as you weed around them*

**2** As the sets grow, you'll need to make sure you keep them free from weeds, which will compete with your crops for nutrients, water, and light. Weed along the rows by hand to avoid damaging your seedlings. Apply a general-purpose fertilizer.

**Tip** Once the plants are larger and less vulnerable, you may want to weed around them using an onion hoe instead, to save time.

**3** The plants will need regular watering as they start to grow. During very dry weather, water them every day. However, take care not to overwater—ensure that the water soaks into the soil rather than sitting on the surface—onions are prone to rotting.

**Careful!** Birds can pull up young seedlings, so cover them with a net if needed (see pp.128–129).

*Use a fine nozzle on your watering can to sprinkle water gently over your plants*

*Harvest your crop when the weather is dry to prevent them from rotting*

4 Most onions will be ready to harvest in late summer, when the leaves wilt and turn yellow. After harvesting, leave the onions to dry in the sun for a few days—on a rack is ideal, so that the air and warmth can surround them.

**Tip** Onions can be stored indoors in a cool, dry location, such as a basement, until you want to use them. Tie the stalks together to form a plait and hang them up.

## Caring for your **Onions**

Grown from sets, onions are one of the easiest kitchen garden vegetables, and with a little care and attention you can be harvesting your own bumper crop in no time.

*Leave onions to dry before storing*

*Remove the dirt and soil before storing onions*

### Things to watch out for...

**Rotting bulbs** A waterlogged soil can cause onions to rot, but another cause could be onion flies. This pest tunnels into the base of the plant, rotting the bulb and eventually causing the plant to collapse. There is no cure once the pest attacks, you will have to dig up all your bulbs and destroy them. Cover young plants with fabric to help deter the pest from laying eggs nearby.

**Rustling skins** You'll know that your onions have been drying long enough and are ready to store once their skins become papery and start to rustle. Clean them thoroughly before you store them so that they will keep as long as possible.

# Grow Garlic

A wonderfully versatile vegetable for cooking, garlic is easy to grow and ideal if you don't have much space, since it will thrive in pots or window boxes. Simply push the cloves into the soil and watch them grow.

full sun

light soil

## Equipment

- Garlic cloves, certified disease-free
- Fork
- Rake
- Bamboo poles
- String
- Dibber
- Watering can
- General-purpose fertilizer
- Trowel

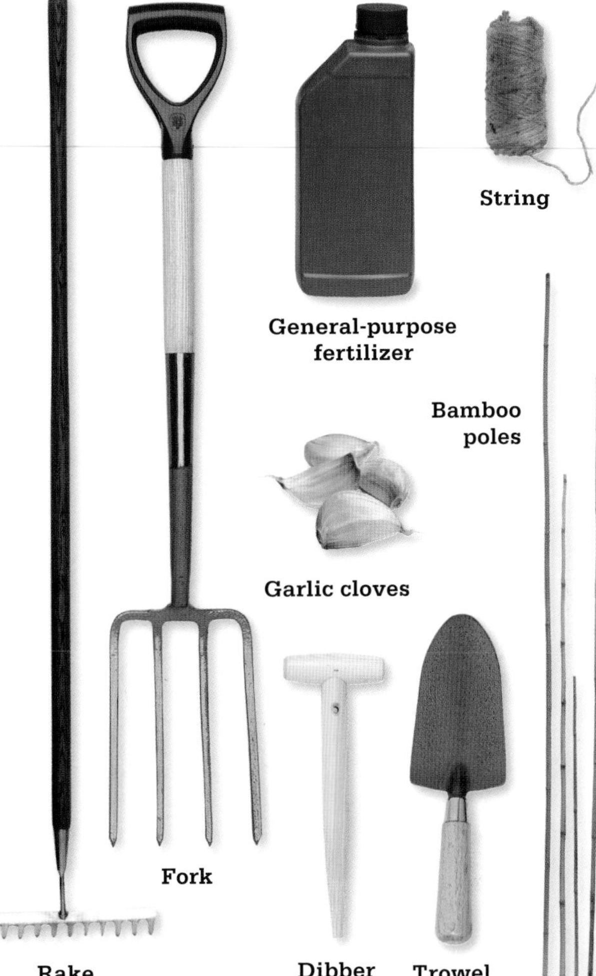

**Garlic** *20–36 weeks until harvest*

**Plant cloves** *in the ground between fall and spring*

**Weed and water** *the seedlings well during summer*

**Harvest** *the bulbs between summer and mid-fall*

**1** Choose garlic cloves that are certified disease-free. Don't use cloves from supermarkets. They may germinate, but some will be varieties from hotter climates and may be unsuitable for cooler conditions. Pull apart the bulbs into individual cloves.

**Tip** They can be planted any time between fall and spring, but cloves planted in the fall usually result in bigger crops.

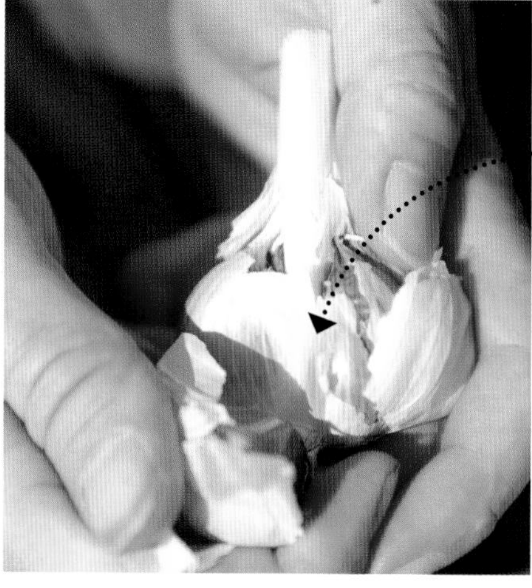

*Break off individual cloves for planting and discard the stem*

*Use a dibber to make the hole*

**2** Don't add manure to the soil before planting because this can rot the bulb. Dig in a balanced fertilizer before planting. Plant the cloves in a sunny spot, with the pointed end facing up and poking slightly out of the ground. Space the cloves 4in (10cm) apart in rows, with a gap of 10in (25cm) between the rows. After planting, water the cloves well.

**3** As the cloves grow, keep the area well weeded to keep other plants from competing with the garlic's shallow roots. Weeds can drastically reduce the yield and size of the bulbs.

**Careful!** Water during dry spells in summer, but avoid excess watering as the bulbs swell; this can cause the garlic to rot.

Bulbs can be gently lifted with a trowel

**4** You can tell that the bulb is ready to harvest when the stems start to turn yellow and fold over. Carefully lift the bulbs, taking care not to bruise or damage them. Leave them to dry in the sun for a few days before taking them inside to store in a cool, dry place.

## Caring for your **Garlic**

Garlic is easy to grow since you don't need to sow seeds. Simply push cloves into the ground and leave them to swell—just be careful not to overwater them.

### Things to watch out for...

**Garden thieves** You may need to protect the cloves after planting since birds are prone to pull them up—construct some secure netting to keep birds at bay (see pp.128–129).

**Orange blisters** A common disease that affects garlic is leek rust, which causes orange, spore-filled blisters on the foliage. There is no cure for this disease, so dig up the plants, destroy them, and ensure that you rotate your crops the following year (see pp.134–135).

After harvesting, garlic can be plaited, as shown here, or stored in a net or a pair of old tights

If stored in a cool, dry place, the bulbs should last for a few months

Avoid hanging the plait in the kitchen unless you plan on using cloves quickly

# Grow Strawberries in a Basket

A hanging basket dripping with glistening red fruit is a lovely sight. If you want to enjoy homegrown strawberries and cream throughout the summer, plant a basket of these delicious berries.

full sun

light soil

## Equipment

- Hanging basket with plastic liner
- General-purpose potting mix
- Controlled-release fertilizer
- Trowel
- 3 strawberry plants
- Watering can
- Wall bracket
- Drill and screws

Hanging basket

General-purpose potting mix

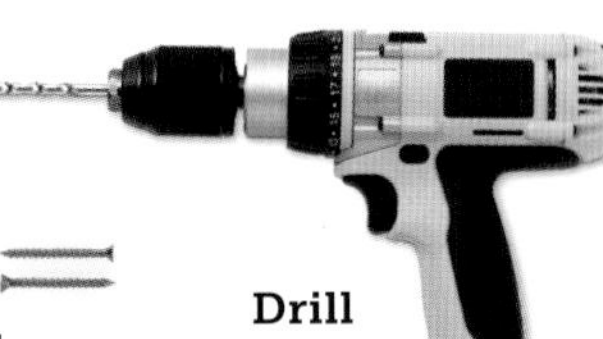

Screws

Drill

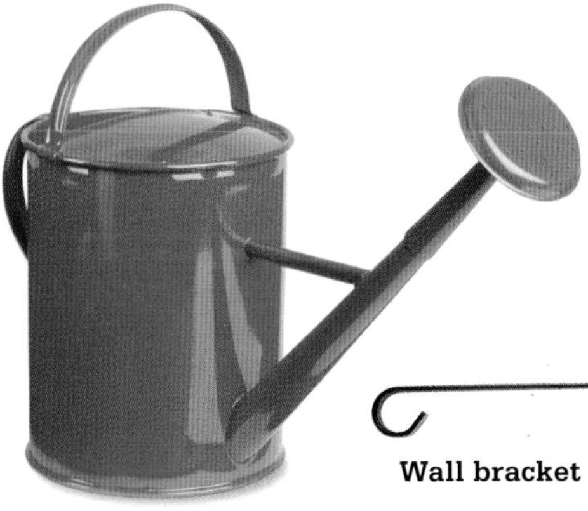

Watering can

Wall bracket

Trowel

Strawberry plants

Controlled-release fertilizer

**Strawberries** *4–6 weeks until harvest*

**Plant out** *in early to mid-spring once all frost has passed*

**Water** *the growing plants well during the summer*

**Harvest** *when ripe, between late spring and mid-fall*

Use scissors to cut several holes in the sides and base of the liner

**1** Choose a large hanging basket with a liner. If the liner does not already have drainage holes, cut them yourself to allow the soil to drain, which will prevent the strawberry plants from rotting.

**Careful!** Ensure you have a sturdy place such as a fence post or wall to hang your basket since it will be very heavy when filled.

**2** Fill the hanging basket with some high-quality, general-purpose potting mix and add a controlled-release fertilizer to keep the plants well supplied with nutrients as they grow.

**Tip** If the basket has a rounded bottom, stand it in a large plant pot to keep it secure as you fill it.

Mix the controlled-release fertilizer with the soil mix

Fill about two-thirds full of mix to leave room for the plants

**3** Plant three strawberry plants so that just the crowns of the plants, the points at which all the stems sprout from, are above the surface of the soil mix. Firm the plants in gently, using your fingertips.

**Tip** Choose one seedling each of early, mid, and late varieties, and you'll have fruit for a longer period.

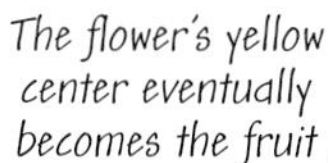

Remove about 50 percent of the flower heads in the first year to allow the plants to establish

The flower's yellow center eventually becomes the fruit

**4** Strawberry plants can produce fruit for more than one year if you want them to. To keep them going, reduce the crop in the first year by removing some of the flowers. When pinching back, snap the flowers off at the base of the stem, taking care not to damage the plant.

**Tip** Some strawberries produce pink flowers, which are an attractive alternative for display.

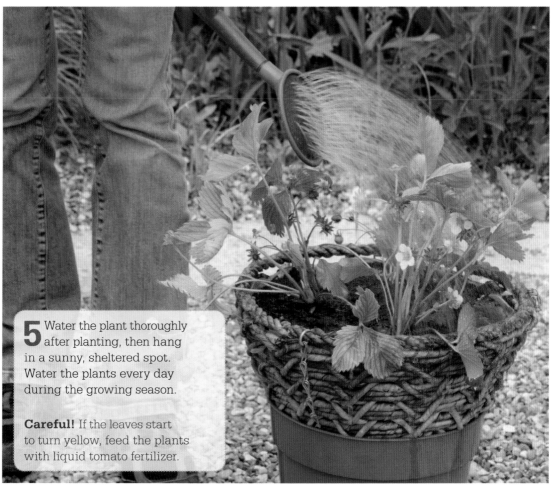

**5** Water the plant thoroughly after planting, then hang in a sunny, sheltered spot. Water the plants every day during the growing season.

**Careful!** If the leaves start to turn yellow, feed the plants with liquid tomato fertilizer.

# Caring for your **Strawberries**

Strawberries are very easy to grow and perfect for a beginner to try; just ensure that you keep them well fed and watered, and keep birds at bay.

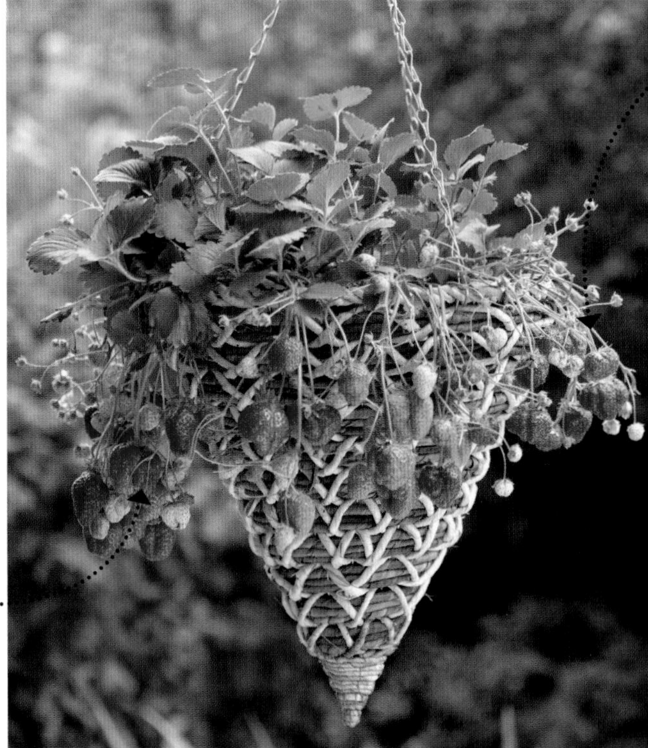

*Fruit will last longer if you include ¾in (2cm) of stem when you pick them*

*Pick strawberries regularly when they turn bright red to keep the fruit coming*

## Things to watch out for...

**Dry soil** During the summer strawberry plants need regular watering and their soil should not be allowed to dry out. Ideally you should also give them a balanced liquid fertilizer once a week.

**Garden thieves** As the fruit starts to ripen, it will become irresistible to pests such as birds and wasps. Place a net over the basket to keep birds out and hang a jelly trap—a jelly jar with some jelly and water in the bottom—nearby to deter wasps.

**The angle of the sun** If you can, turn the hanging basket every few days to ensure that light reaches all parts of the plants. This will encourage the fruit to swell and ripen.

**Old foliage** To keep the plants fruiting for the following year, cut back the old foliage after harvesting, leaving just new, young leaves.

**Also learn to grow** ▸▸▸

# How to grow **Tumbling Tomatoes**

full sun

light soil

## Equipment

- 3 trailing tomato plants
- Hanging basket with good drainage
- General-purpose potting mix
- Controlled-release fertilizer
- Watering can

### TRAILING TOMATOES

**Trailing, or tumbling, tomatoes** are a wonderful savory alternative to strawberries for a hanging basket and are just as easy to grow. Growing them in hanging baskets keeps them away from slugs and allows you to pick the fruit comfortably. Position the basket close to the kitchen for convenience.

### PLANTING

**Partially fill the hanging basket** with high-quality potting mix and add in controlled-release fertilizer at the recommended rate. Arrange three trailing tomatoes around the edge of the basket, fill around them with soil, firm in, and water well.

**Keep the plants well watered** and fertilize regularly with tomato fertilizer. The plants will tumble down as they grow. Pick the tomatoes as they ripen—depending on the variety, this could be in as little as a few months. Tomatoes are annual plants, so remove the plants after cropping and add them to the compost heap.

### RIPENING

**If you want to speed up the ripening process** while the tomatoes are still growing outside, you can place banana skins on the surface of the soil mix in the hanging basket. A chemical naturally produced by this fruit will rapidly color up your tomatoes.

**Harvest all remaining tomatoes** before the first fall frost. Don't worry if the tomatoes are green—they will ripen on the windowsill inside. Alternatively, you can make fried green tomatoes.

### TROUBLESHOOTING

**Watch out for** tomato blight, which is a fungus that spreads among the foliage and will quickly kill the plants. Remove foliage that is turning brown as soon as you spot it and dispose of it immediately.

# How to **Carry Out Basic Plant Care**

It is important to take regular care of your plants. They will need watering, feeding, and protection from pests and diseases. Seedlings should be kept free from competing weeds. Look after your plants well, and they will reward you with bumper crops to harvest later in the year.

## Pests and disease

Keep an eye out for any diseased plant material and remove it as soon as you see it. Monitor leaves and crops for signs of damage from pests such as aphids and remove them before the problem spreads. Plants bred to be resistant to diseases are available, but healthy, well-fed plants will be less likely to attract pests and fall prey to diseases.

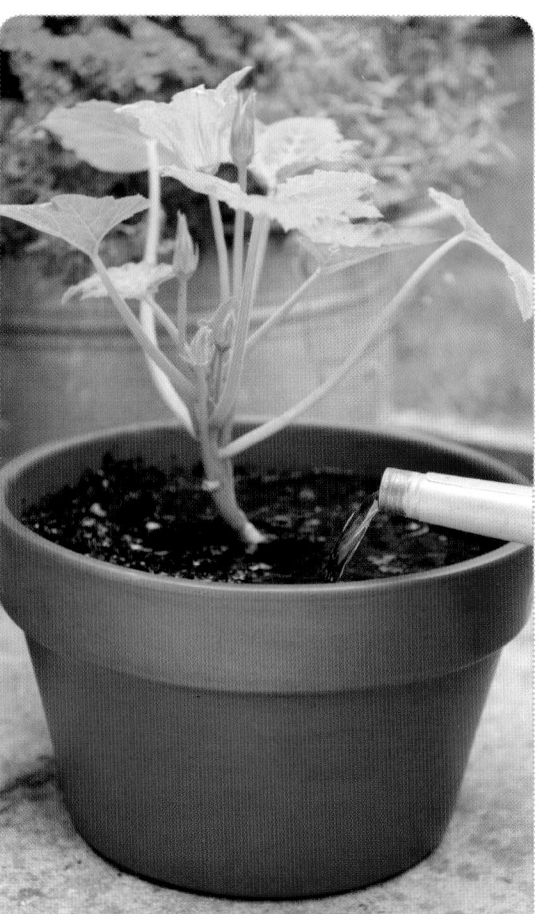

## Regular watering

Keep plants well watered so that they remain strong and healthy and are able to resist disease. In warm conditions, such as greenhouses and on window ledges, emerging seedlings will need watering at least once a day. Crops in containers will need more frequent watering than those in garden beds since pots will drain faster.

# How to **Protect Plants from Slugs**

These silent, slimy pests can be devastating since they devour almost any green foliage they come across, munching their way through the vegetable patch, particularly at night and in moist, damp conditions. Don't worry though, there are plenty of ways to deal with them.

Check foliage regularly to ensure it hasn't been munched

**Place grit or sand around the plants**

This beer trap attracts slugs, which fall into the jar and cannot escape
These collars protect the plants from slugs


**Place slug collars around plants**

## Slug-proofing your plants

Placing a barrier of grit or sand around your seedlings will deter slugs because they don't like the sharp, dry texture. Slug collars, which can be bought at the garden center, will also discourage slugs and snails, while pots filled with beer will lure slugs in and trap them. Copper tape placed around the rim of pots gives a slight static shock to slugs that try to cross it, and slug pellets are also effective. Choose whichever option suits you best.

# How to **Feed**

Fertilizing your plants regularly will keep them healthy and maximize your crop. There is a variety of fertilizers available, which should be applied to your plants at crucial stages of their growth and fruit production. It is also important to regularly replenish the nutrients the plants take from the soil by digging in well-rotted manure.

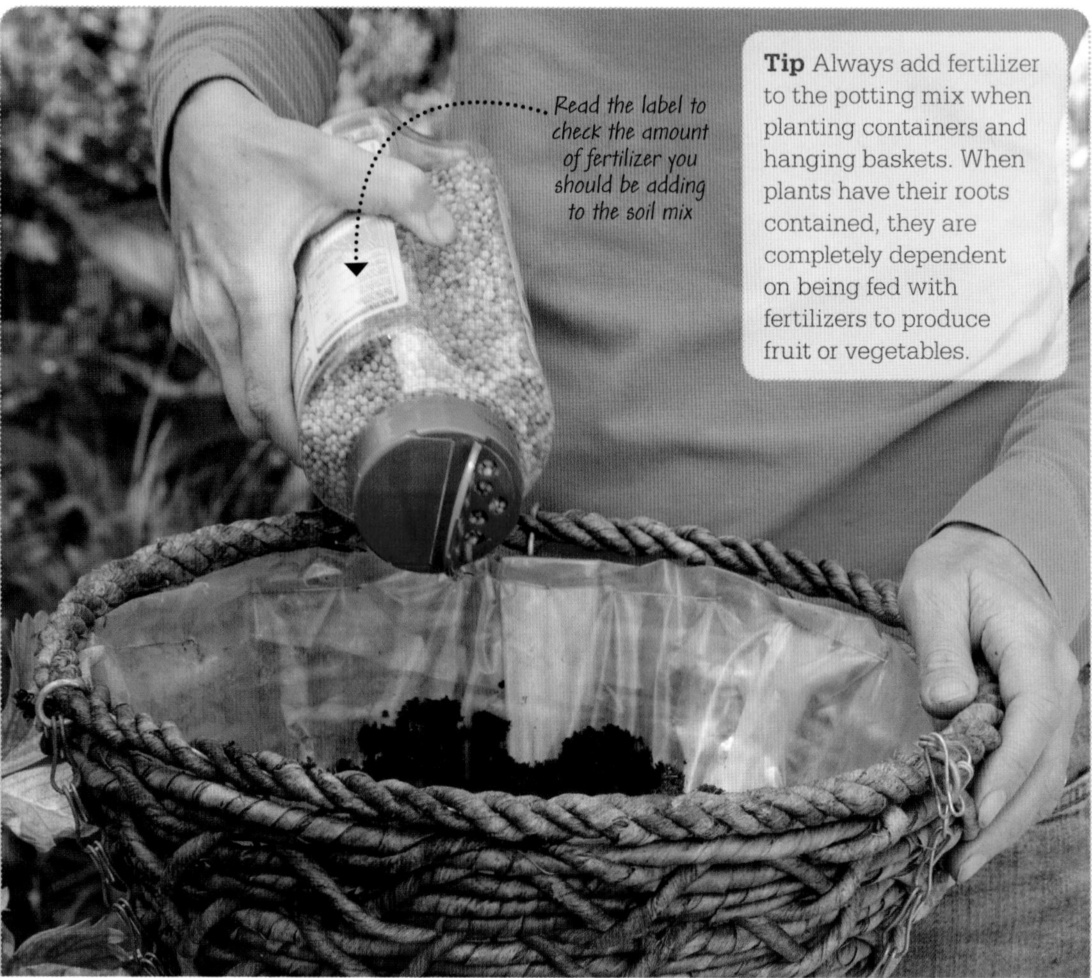

Read the label to check the amount of fertilizer you should be adding to the soil mix


**Tip** Always add fertilizer to the potting mix when planting containers and hanging baskets. When plants have their roots contained, they are completely dependent on being fed with fertilizers to produce fruit or vegetables.

## Feeding

To boost crops, use a general fertilizer with balanced amounts of nitrogen, phosphorus, and potassium (see pp.24–25). A fertilizer high in potassium will encourage a larger number of fruit on your plants and is especially useful for "hungry" crops such as tomatoes, peppers, and cabbage, which benefit from extra feeds. Controlled-release fertilizer is expensive, but releases the required nutrients when the plant needs them throughout the year.

# How to **Weed**

Don't give weeds a chance to swamp your plants because they may block out light and will take moisture and nutrients from the soil. It is important to remove any weeds from your site before you sow or plant—they can reproduce prolifically and some can root deep into the soil, making them difficult to remove once crops are in place.

Make sure no perennial roots remain—these will quickly regenerate
Use a fork to dislodge larger weeds because a spade can cut the roots, causing them to multiply

Look out for small weeds that will compete with the seedlings for nutrients
Pull out weeds by hand that are close to seedlings to avoid damaging the plants
Small weeds in the soil or in containers are best removed by hand


## Weeding

Even though you will have weeded your site when you prepared to plant (see p.15), you will still need to weed regularly, especially in the summer months. It is vital that annual weeds, such as groundsel, do not have a chance to set seed and that perennial weeds, such as dandelions, do not take hold. Weed between the rows using a fork or rake, taking care not to damage the plants, or for smaller rows of seedlings, pull out the weeds by hand.

# 2

# Build On It

This chapter will show you how to build on the skills and techniques you have learned so far, and extend the range of tasty culinary treats you can grow yourself.

**In this section learn to grow:**

**Potatoes**
*see pp.78–81*

**Zucchini**
*see pp.82–85*

**Peppers**
*see pp.88–92*

**Carrots**
*see pp.94–97*

**Cabbage**
*see pp.100-104*

**Beans**
*see pp.106–110*

**Raspberries**
*see pp.112–115*

**Apples**
*see pp.116–120*

**Currants**
*see pp.122–125*

# How to **Sow in Furrows and Thin Out**

Seeds that can be sown directly into the ground are most commonly sown in furrows. To create your furrow, insert stakes where you want it to start and end, and then tie a piece of garden twine or string between them. With the string as a guide, use a hoe to create a shallow trench between the stakes—this is where you will sow your seeds.

**Sowing**

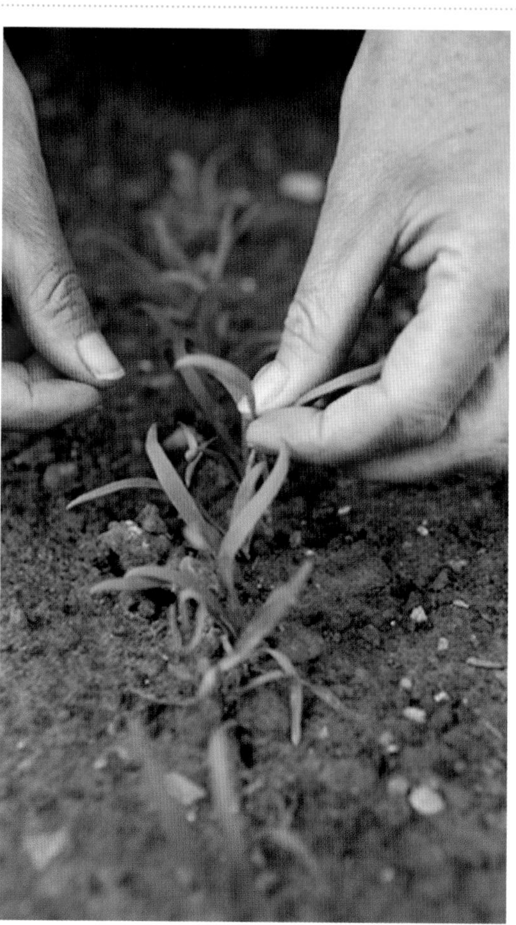

**Thinning out**

## Getting your seeds started

Water the furrow, then sprinkle the seeds into it at the spacing given on the seed packet. Gently cover the seeds with soil, then water in well. Once the seeds germinate and show their first true leaves, thin them out by hand, leaving the strongest to keep growing. It is important to do this so that your seedlings are not competing for water, light, and nutrients. The ideal distance between them will vary for each crop, so always check the seed packet.

# How to **Repot**

Plants that were sown indoors and have begun to outgrow their pots but can't be moved outdoors because conditions are still too cold will need to be repotted—put into a new, larger pot to maintain healthy growth. Make sure you use fresh potting mix recommended for seed sowing.

Gently squeeze the pot to loosen the soil mix, making it easy to remove your seedling
Look at the root system to see if there is room for the plant to grow

**Repotting seedlings**

Hold the seedling gently by its leaves, never by its stem
Use a pencil or a dibber to tease the seedling's roots from the soil mix

**Separating seedlings**

## Dividing and repotting

Seedlings are ready to be repotted when their roots begin to fill their pots and when their first leaves have expanded and new leaves are beginning to develop between them. Partially fill your new, larger pot with fresh potting mix and give it a good watering. Gently remove your seedling from its pot and replant it. Seedlings grown in seed flats will also need separating and replanting—gently pull them apart and plant them in individual pots.

# How to **Harden Off and Protect from Cold**

Cold temperatures can cause your crops to shrivel and die, so it's important to both prepare and protect them. Plants that have been grown indoors and have tender leaves will need to be hardened off before they are planted outside, otherwise they may be damaged by frost or strong winds.

**Harden off outside**

**Harden off on the porch**

## Hardening off

To prepare your crops for cooler outdoor temperatures, place them outside during the day and bring them inside at night for two weeks. Alternatively, place them in a cold frame for a few days or even just on the porch if no frost is forecast. This will allow the plants to adjust and slowly acclimatize to the temperature. After this they will be ready to plant out but may still need further protection, so keep an eye on the weather.

## Homemade cloches

Crops that have been planted out may still need protection from the weather if frost is threatened. Cloches help prevent plants from being damaged by cold weather because they serve as miniature greenhouses, trapping warm air around the plant, with the added bonus of also protecting them against pests. Cut away the bases of see-through plastic bottles to make your own.

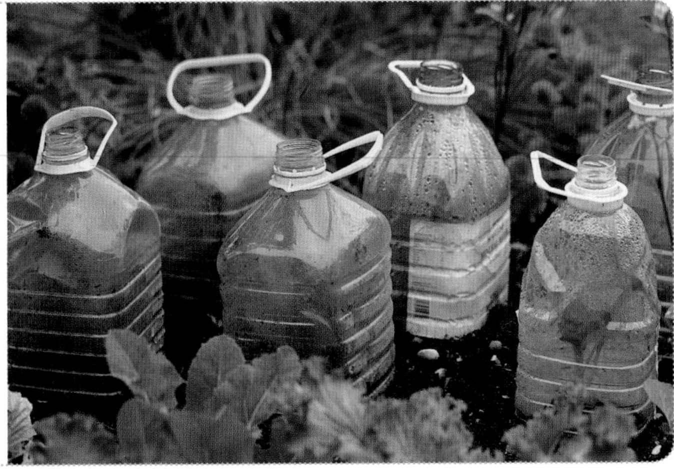

## Manufactured cloches

Seeds that have been sown outside will need protection from cold weather, and a manufactured glass or plastic cloche can do just that. Large cloches like this can also be used to warm up the soil before seeds are sown, to ensure your crops the best possible start. Simply place the cloche in position a few weeks before you plan to sow.

## Cold frames

Whether you buy one or make one, cold frames look attractive in the garden and provide protection for vegetables that are in pots or containers. The low wooden structures have a transparent lid of glass or plastic and give plants protection from the cold, while also allowing them essential light.

# How to **Mulch**

Mulching involves covering the soil around your plants with a generous layer of material such as manure, compost, or bark chips to suppress weeds, retain moisture, and improve the soil quality. Straw can also be used as a mulch to lift strawberries off the soil and keep plants well ventilated.

**Straw**

**Bark chips**

**Compost**

**Well-rotted manure**

## Mulching

Outdoor plants should be mulched in springtime, after planting and watering. Biodegradable mulches such as compost, manure, or leaf mold break down to release nutrients into the soil and help it to retain moisture. Be careful to keep compost off the foliage though, since it can damage it. Non-biodegradable mulches such as pebbles or decorative gravel are often used and can be an attractive addition to the garden.

# How to **Stake**

Supporting crops with bamboo poles or wooden stakes will prevent tall or top-heavy plants, such as broccoli, or those that are heavily burdened with fruit or vegetables, such as peppers or tomatoes, from collapsing, which would risk the health of the plant and its crop.

**Careful positioning**

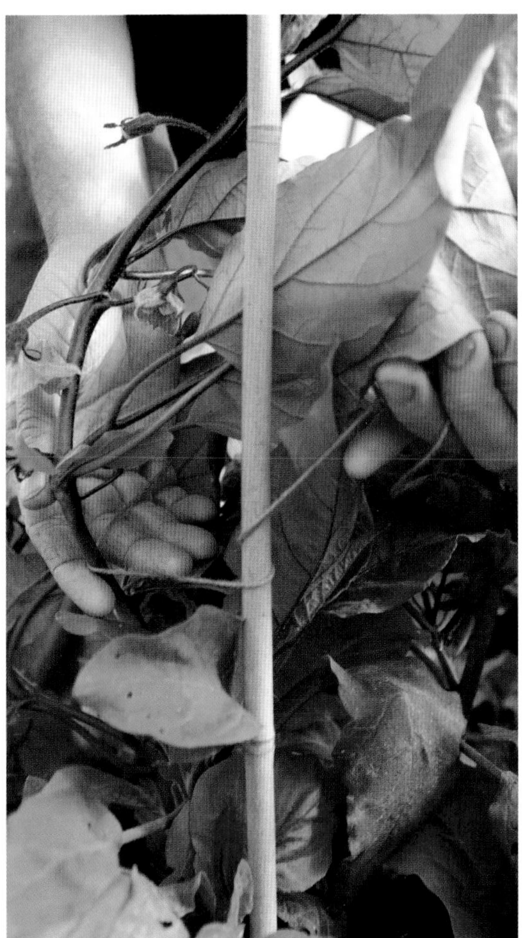

**Tying the stake**

## Staking

Insert your bamboo pole or wooden stake into the soil so that it is close to the main stem of your plant, but be careful not to damage the roots as you do so. Ensure that it is stable and vertical. Using garden twine or string, tie your plants to their stakes using figure-eight knots (see p.34). Keep an eye on the plants as they develop and add more supports if you need to. Some plants, such as runner beans, will require staking from a very early stage.

# Grow Potatoes in a Tub

Potatoes are the staple vegetable for many aspiring kitchen gardeners. Not only are they easy to grow, but planting tubers in large containers is also a simple way to produce a bumper crop even if you don't have much space.

full sun

moist soil

## Equipment

- Potato tubers
- Egg carton
- Deep container
  such a large tub, with drainage holes
- Crocks
- General-purpose potting mix
- Trowel
- Watering can

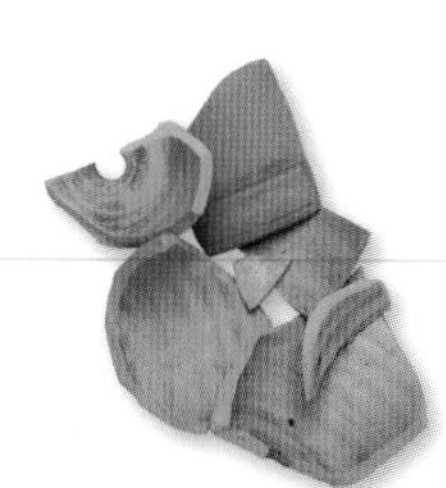
Crocks

General-purpose potting mix

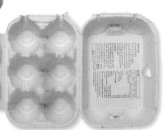

Potato tubers

Trowel

Watering can

Egg carton

Deep container

**Potatoes** *12–22 weeks until harvest*

**Chit potatoes** *in a cool place in early to mid-spring*

**Plant out** *your potatoes in early to mid-spring*

**Hill up** *the growing plants during summer*

**Harvest** *during the summer and into the fall*

**1** Most potatoes benefit from being chitted in early spring. Chitting is the process of sprouting the potatoes before planting. Put potato tubers in an egg carton, with the end with the most sprouts or eyes facing upward. Place the carton on a window ledge to sprout the shoots.

**Tip** The potatoes are ready to plant after a few weeks, when the shoots are about ¾in (2cm) long.

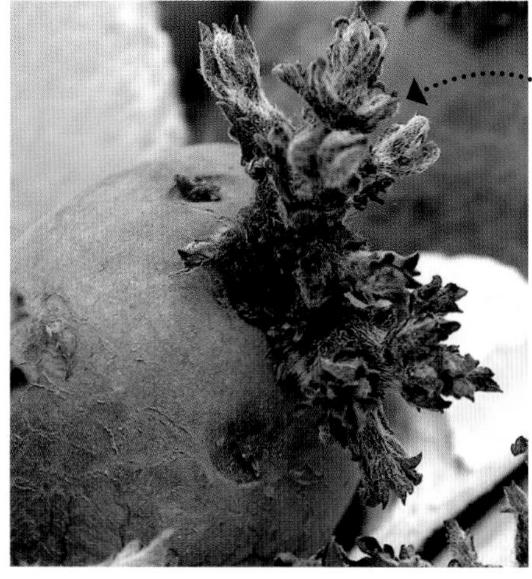

These chits will get the potatoes growing quickly once placed in the soil

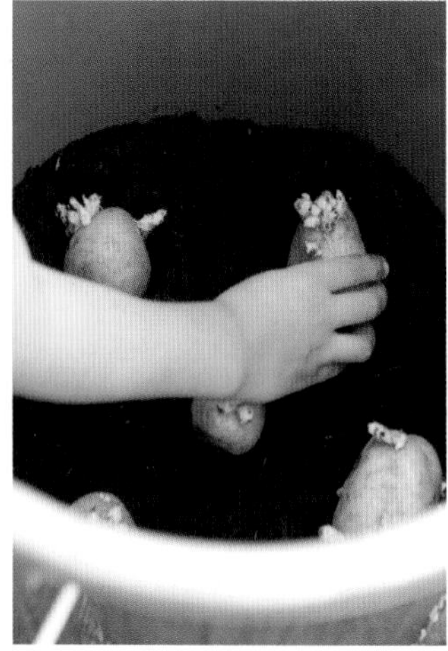

**2** Choose a large container or a plastic bin with drainage holes—if it doesn't have any you'll need to create some yourself—and fill it a third full with general-purpose potting mix. Evenly space five potatoes in the container. Cover the potatoes with mix so the container is two-thirds full.

**Tip** Main potatoes can be grown in tubs if you just plant two or three tubers instead of five.

**3** Place the container in a sunny, sheltered location. The potatoes will need to be earthed up as they grow. This means packing potting mix around the plants, leaving the top few leaves uncovered, until it reaches the top of the container.

**Why?** Earthing up keeps light from reaching the tubers so they don't turn green and inedible, and it also helps to increase the yield.

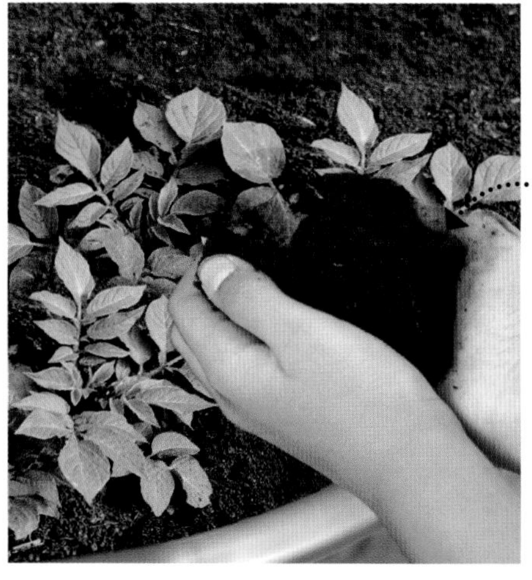

Make sure that the tubers are not exposed to sunlight until they are ready to harvest

**4** Keep the plants well watered as they grow and make sure they are not allowed to dry out. Potatoes will be ready to harvest just as they finish flowering; dig one up to check if it is ready. To harvest, tip the container upside down and pick out the potatoes.

**Tip** Harvest on a dry day, and leave the tubers out in the sunshine for a few hours.

## Caring for your **Potatoes**

Growing potatoes in a tub makes them much less susceptible to pests and diseases than those grown in the garden—just don't let the tubers see the light.

### Things to watch out for...

**Dying flowers** Once your flowers start to die, it is time to harvest. Early potatoes are best eaten immediately but main crops and salad potatoes can be stored for longer in a cool, dark place. See p.185 for details on storage.

**Green tubers** If the potatoes are exposed to daylight they become green and inedible and should not be eaten. Take care to earth up plants deeply to avoid this.

**Patchy, rotten foliage** Potato blight is a fungus that causes the leaves of potato plants to rot, before spreading to the tubers. Remove and destroy any infected foliage, and choose resistant varieties in future years.

*Take care not to pierce your potatoes when harvesting with a fork*

# Grow Zucchini in a Bag

Zucchini are very easy plants to grow if you provide them with the conditions they need—give them plenty of sun, water, and an abundance of potting mix, and you will be harvesting crops all summer long. Growing them in a planting bag is ideal if your garden space is limited.

full sun

moist soil

## Equipment

- Zucchini seeds
- Small plastic pots
- General-purpose potting mix
- Dibber
- Planting bag
- Crocks
- Trowel
- Gloves
- Watering can
- Liquid fertilizer

Small plastic pots

Trowel

General-purpose potting mix

Crocks

Dibber

Gloves

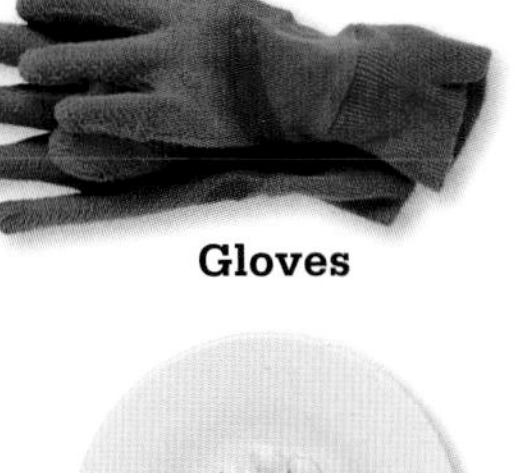

Watering can

Liquid fertilizer

Zucchini seeds

Planting bag

**Zucchini** *14 weeks until harvest*

**Sow your seeds** *in mid-spring under cover*

**Harden off** *in late spring to early summer*

**Water** *the growing plants throughout summer*

**Harvest** *from midsummer to mid-fall*

**1** Zucchini seeds should be sown in mid-spring. Fill small plastic pots with general-purpose potting mix. Use a dibber to create a hole and sow one seed per pot, 1in (2.5cm) deep. Place on a sunny windowsill to germinate.

**Tip** Place the seed on its side to keep it from rotting in the pot—water can run off it rather than collect on its wide surface.

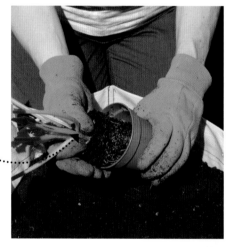

*Be careful not to damage the stem*

**2** Once the risk of frost is over in late spring or early summer, harden the plants off (see p.74). Create holes in the bottom of the planting bag, move it into a sunny, sheltered spot, and then fill it with high-quality, general purpose potting mix, leaving a gap of about 4in (10cm) at the top. Water the zucchini well and then ease it out of its pot gently, being careful not to damage the roots.

**3** Make a small hole in the middle of the planting bag and plant the zucchini so that the base of the plant is level with the top of the soil mix. Firm the plant in well using your fingers.

**Tip** If you mix the soil mix with well-rotted manure, you will give a further boost to the hungry plant.

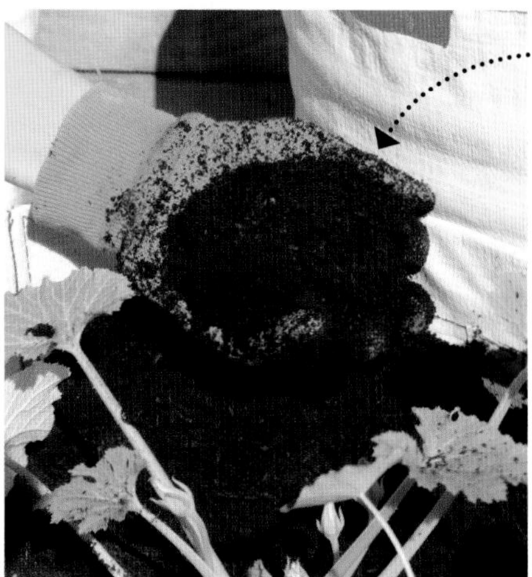

*Wear gloves when handling soil mix, manure, or fertilizers*

**4** Water the plant in well. Zucchini are hungry plants and will need feeding with liquid fertilizer every couple of weeks.

**Careful!** Once the zucchini are ready to harvest, pick regularly; if zucchini are left on the plant, they will swell up to an overlarge size and the plant will stop producing other fruit.

Avoid watering at midday—this can scorch the leaves

## Caring for your **Zucchini**

Zucchini are heavy croppers, virtually trouble-free, and incredibly versatile—they can be grown in bags, directly in the soil, or even on top of a compost heap.

Turn the bags regularly to ensure all the zucchini receive sunlight

Zucchini are annual plants, so remove them after they have finished cropping and add to the compost heap

### Things to watch out for...

**Colorful blooms** Beautiful zucchini flowers taste delicious fried up as fritters. Harvest a few while the plant is growing, but don't remove them all, or you won't get any zucchini. They can be stored in the refrigerator in a sealed bag for a few days.

**Grayish, moldy leaves** Zucchini are generally disease-free, but they can suffer from mildew if their roots get dry; this causes mold to form on the upper surfaces of the leaves. Remove any infected leaves and water the plants well. Since the plants here are grown in bags, they will be prone to dry out quicker than if they were in the ground.

**Also learn to grow ▸▸▸**

# How to grow **Pumpkins and Large Squashes**

**full sun**

**moist soil**

## Equipment

- Pumpkin or squash seeds
- 4-in (10-cm) plastic pots
- Spade
- Well-rotted manure or compost
- Trowel
- Watering can

These large vegetables need lots of time to grow so they will not be ready until late in the season—just in time for fall and winter feasts.

### LOCATION

**Both crops need full sun** and a rich, fertile soil. Pumpkins can be trained up fences or walls; squashes will grow in containers or growing bags.

### SOWING

**In your pots**, sow individual seeds on their sides to discourage decay and cover them up with soil mix. When the risk of frost is over, plant out the seedlings at a distance of 5ft (1.5m) for pumpkins and 3ft (1m) for squashes. Keep them well watered.

**To grow a larger pumpkin**, choose a large variety and remove all flowers except one per plant. A liquid fertilizer each week will encourage good growth.

### HARVESTING

**Pumpkins and squashes** should be left on the vine for as long as possible to allow the skins to harden. This will prevent them from rotting in storage. Harvest when the fruit are large and swollen and leave the pumpkins in a sunny spot to ripen further. Both can be stored in a cool, well-ventilated area for around six months.

**Pumpkin**

**Squash**

# How to grow **Winter and Summer Squashes**

full sun

moist soil

**Winter squash**

## Equipment

- Winter or summer squash seeds
- Spade or trowel
- Well-rotted manure or compost
- Watering can
- Bottle cloche

Both winter and summer squashes come in a wide range of shapes, sizes, and colors, and can liven up any vegetable patch.

### SOWING

**Sow winter squash seeds** directly into rich, fertile soil in late spring. Sow pairs of seeds 1¼in (3cm) deep and 3ft (1m) apart. Use a bottle cloche to cover them. Keep them well watered.

**Summer squash seeds are sown** directly into the soil, 18in (45cm) apart, after the risk of frost has passed. The plants are thirsty and will need almost constant watering as they grow.

### GROWING

**These trailing plants** can be trained up stakes or a trellis. Winter squashes are ideal for growing on the ground among taller plants such as sweet corn, and for smothering out weeds.

### HARVESTING

**Summer squashes** will be ready to harvest from midsummer; winter squashes in late fall to winter. Summer squashes can be harvested early when they are small or left to grow larger for roasting or stuffing. The longer you leave a summer squash on the vine, the thicker its skin will become and the longer it will store. Winter squashes store well in a cool, well-ventilated place.

**Summer squash**

# Grow Peppers in a Pot

In colors ranging from purple and yellow to green, one or two pepper plants can provide plenty for a family throughout the summer. They are ideal for containers and hardly take up any space, so try growing these mild- or spicy-flavored, crunchy vegetables for yourself.

full sun

moist soil

## Equipment

- Pepper seeds
- Plastic pots—small and large
- General-purpose potting mix
- Trowel
- Propagator
- Bamboo poles
- String
- Watering can
- Pruners
- Gloves
- High-potassium liquid fertilizer

**Pepper seeds**

**General-purpose potting mix**

**Propagator**

**String**

**Bamboo poles**

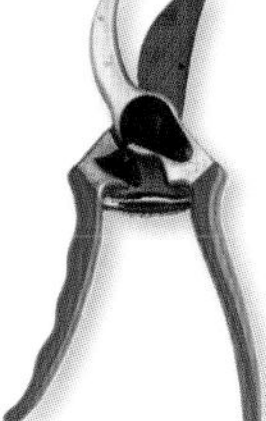
**Pruners**

**Liquid fertilizer**

**Watering can**

**Trowel**

**Plastic pots**

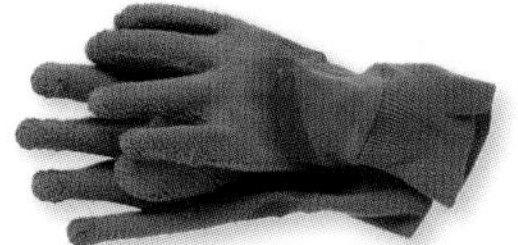
**Gloves**

**Peppers** *20–26 weeks until harvest*

**Sow** *seed in early to mid-spring and place in a propagator*

**Plant out** *in early summer, after the frost has passed*

**Water** *the growing plants well as they develop peppers*

**Harvest** *in summer through to the end of the fall*

**1** Pepper plants are tender and require a long growing season, so sow them indoors in early spring to give them a good start. Sow seeds individually in small plastic pots filled with general-purpose potting mix. Cover the seeds with a thin layer of mix and place the pots in a heated propagator set to around 68–75°F (20–24°C) for a week or two.

Sow only one seed in each pot

Gently remove the plant from its pot, being careful not to damage the roots

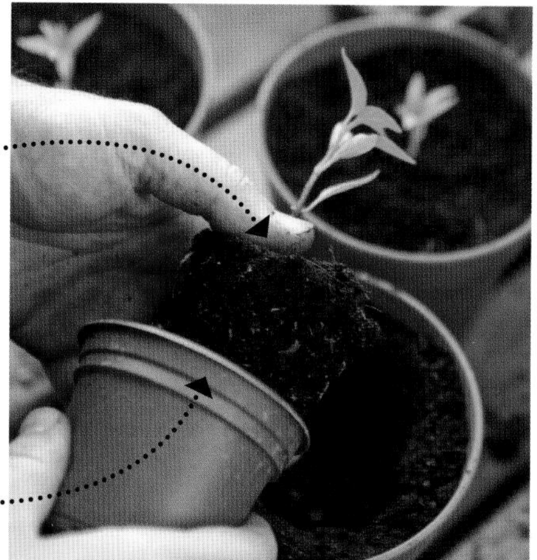

Check to see if there is a healthy root system

**2** Peppers are ready to be repotted when their roots start showing through the holes in the bottom of the pot. Select some of the strongest seedlings, bearing in mind that you will only need about two or three plants for the year, and pot them up into 3½-in (9-cm) plastic pots.

**Tip** Give the plants a feed with a high-potassium tomato fertilizer.

**3** When the seedlings reach about 8in (20cm) tall, they should again be repotted into larger pots to give the plants more space to grow. It is important for the plants to get as strong and healthy as possible before being transferred outside.

**Tip** Pinch back the plants when they reach 8in (20cm) tall, to encourage them to branch out.

Make sure to water the plant well to keep it growing strong

These flowers will eventually develop into peppers

**4** Peppers can be grown in a greenhouse, but if they are to be planted outside, you will need to harden the plants off by leaving them outdoors during the day and bringing them in at night for a couple of weeks (see p.74). Once the plants have been hardened off, they can be planted into growing bags, containers, or directly into the soil at a spacing of 15in (40cm) apart.

**5** As the plants grow, they will need staking. Insert a stout bamboo pole into each pot near the base of the plant, being careful not to damage the roots. Tie the plant to it using garden twine in a figure-eight knot (see p.34). When the first fruit appears, start feeding the plants with a high-potassium liquid fertilizer each week.

Make sure the stake is firmly "planted" in the pot
Keep tying the plant to the stake as it grows

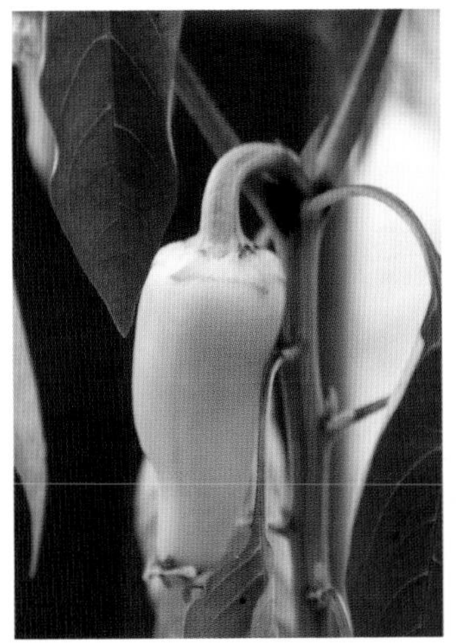

**6** When fruit starts ripening, they will first turn green and then red, yellow, purple, or orange, depending on the variety chosen. Use a sharp pair of pruners to remove them from the plants.

**Tip** It is important to harvest them promptly so that the plant can devote its energy to ripening the remaining peppers.

# Caring for your **Peppers**

These tender plants need to get off to an early start because they require a long ripening period. Feed them regularly and stake them to keep them strong and healthy.

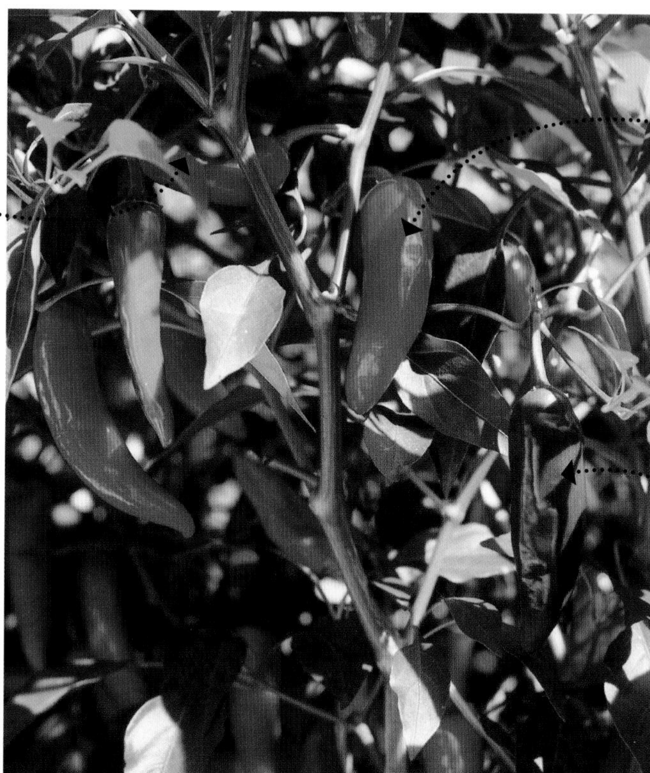

If the leaves are looking yellow, give the plants a high-potassium liquid fertilizer

Fruit will change from green to red or yellow as they ripen

Throw a cloche over the plant if fruit haven't ripened before fall

## Things to watch out for...

**Indoor plants** If you are growing peppers indoors, they will need to be pollinated by hand, since flying insects won't be able to access the flowers to cross-pollinate them. Brush the insides of the flowers with a small paintbrush to pass the pollen from one flower to another. If you are growing in a greenhouse, remember to open vents and doors on hot days to keep plants well ventilated, and wet the door down with a sponge and moisten the floors to keep moisture levels up.

**Garden pests** Although peppers are affected by few diseases, there are pests that might trouble your crops, such as aphids. These pests can swarm a plant and cover it with sticky honeydew, on which mold can grow. Apply an appropriate insecticide to control them.

**Tall plants with few sideshoots** The tips of the seedlings should be pinched back when they are about 8in (20cm) tall. This will encourage the plant to produce more fruiting sideshoots.

**Also learn to grow ▸▸▸**

# How to grow **Sweet corn**

full sun

light soil

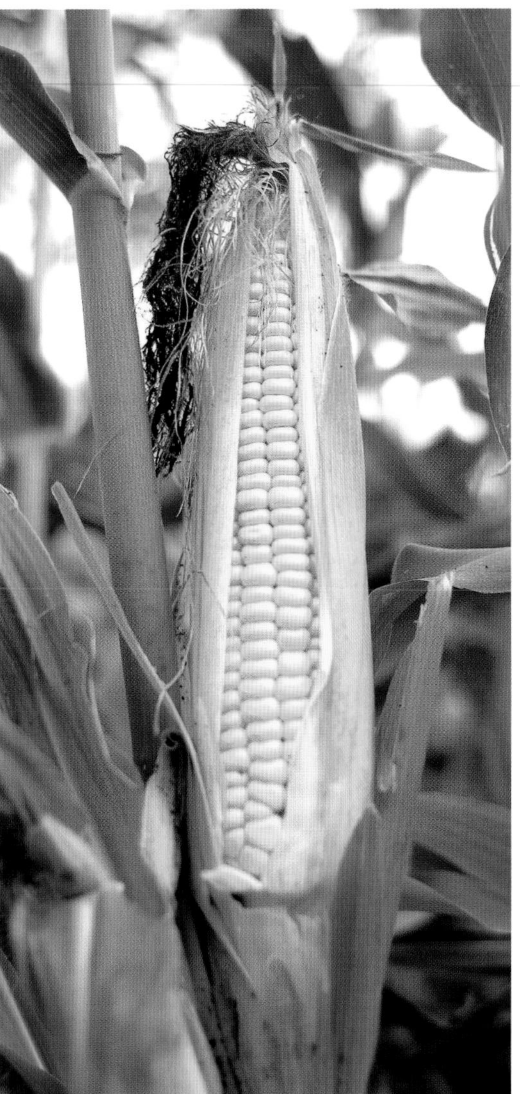

## Equipment

- Sweet corn seeds
- 3½-in (9-cm) plastic pots
- General-purpose potting mix
- Trowel
- Bamboo poles and string

### SOWING

**Start sweet corn off under cover** in mid-spring, sowing individual seeds into 3½-in (9-cm) pots. Keep them on a sunny windowsill or greenhouse bench. When the risk of cold is over, prepare your soil thoroughly and harden the plants off (see p.74).

**Plant the sweet corn in blocks** or grids rather than single rows. They are wind-pollinated, and planting them closely in blocks ensures that pollen will pass from one plant to another, giving you high yields. Water the plants well after planting out and keep watering them regularly throughout the summer months, especially as the cobs develop.

### STAKING

**Stake the plants** as they start to get taller, using poles and string (see p.77), and mound up the bases with soil to make them more sturdy.

### TROUBLESHOOTING

**Keep an eye out for badgers and deer**, which can devour an entire crop overnight. Cover the plants with netting to protect them from birds.

### HARVESTING

**To check whether the sweet corn is ready** for harvesting, peel back the green sheath and press a thumbnail into one of the kernels. If milky sap spurts out, it is ready for harvesting. Sweet corn is an annual crop, so dig up the plants after they've cropped and add them to the compost heap.

### PLANT COMBINATIONS

**Grow squash** in between the taller sweet corn plants because they will help to suppress weeds.

# Grow Carrots in a Bag

This deliciously sweet and crunchy crop is a kitchen staple. The roots will need a light, well-drained soil to grow straight and smooth, and the plants will need protection from carrot rust fly pests. Grow them in deep containers and keep them close to the kitchen for convenience.

**full sun** **light soil**

## Equipment

- Carrot seeds
- Deep container
- General-purpose potting mix
- Trowel
- Bamboo poles
- Insect-proof netting
- Watering can

Carrot seeds

General-purpose potting mix

Insect-proof netting

Bamboo poles

Watering can

Trowel

Deep container

**Carrots** *12–20 weeks until harvest*

**Sow** *seed from mid-spring onward after the risk of frost has passed*

**Thin** *the seedlings after a few weeks in mid- to late spring*

**Harvest crops** *throughout summer and into fall*

**1** Ensure that your container has drainage holes and then fill it with potting mix. Add in an all-purpose fertilizer and create a seed furrow by pressing a piece of bamboo lightly across the surface, ½in (1cm) deep. If space allows, create another furrow 6in (15cm) away from the first.

**Tip** If you do not have a piece of bamboo, use a pen or pencil.

Make the furrow no deeper than ½in (1cm)

**2** Using all the seeds in the packet, sow thinly along the furrows. Lightly brush back the soil to fill in the furrow, being careful not to disturb the seeds. Water them in well using a watering can with a fine nozzle.

**3** After a few weeks the seeds should have germinated, but they will need thinning out so that the strongest can grow to full size (see p.72). Thin to leave the plants 1½in (4cm) apart.

**Careful!** Thin crops in the early morning or evening, when carrot rust flies are least active (see next page); they are attracted to the plants' scent, which is released when their leaves are disturbed.

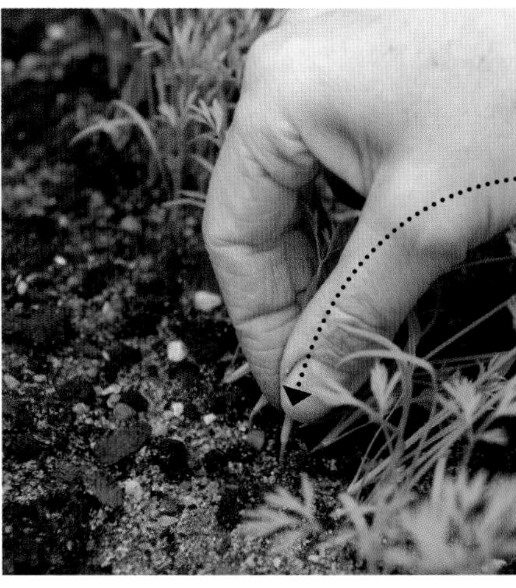

The thinnings from carrots can be replanted in another bed

Select varieties that are less susceptible to carrot rust flies, though none are totally resistant
Carrot rust flies cannot fly higher than about 24in (60cm)

**4** To prevent attack by carrot rust flies (see below), create a barrier of fabric that, together with the pot, is 24in (60cm) high; carrot rust flies are low-flying and will not be able to fly over it and lay eggs nearby. Alternatively, lift the container so that it is the same height off the ground.

**Tip** Weed around the carrots as they grow, being careful not to disturb the plants.

# Caring for your **Carrots**

As long as you can protect them from carrot rust flies and give them a regular supply of water, carrots are easy crops to grow and can be harvested in as little as 12 weeks.

## Things to watch out for...

**Carrot rust flies** These pests are a persistent problem for carrots. Larvae tunnel into the roots, making them unsightly and inedible. Thin in the early morning or evening, erect fabric guards around the plants, and choose resistant varieties such as 'Flyaway'. Alternatively, try growing strong-scented plants such as onions next to them to mask their scent.

**Crooked roots** If there are rocks or clumps of hard clay in your soil, carrot roots may become misshapen; they prefer light, sandy soils, which allow long roots to develop.

**Unused space** Carrots will be ready to harvest about 12 weeks after sowing. To make the most of your space and to give yourself a steady supply of carrots, make small sowings throughout the growing season—this will also help to ensure you don't end up with a glut.

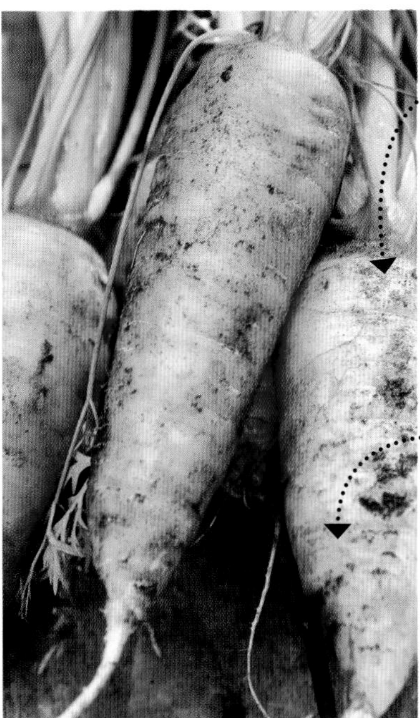
Ripe carrots should measure about 1½in (4cm) across
On heavy or rocky soil, choose stump-rooted or round carrots that taste delicious as well

**Also learn to grow ▸▸▸**

# How to grow **Turnips and Beets**

full sun

light soil

## Equipment

- Turnip or beet seeds
- Cell flat
- Dibber
- Trowel
- Bamboo poles and string
- Fork and rake
- Watering can

Beets are easy to grow and are a delicious, colorful addition to any salad. Grow turnips for their tasty roots and for their leaves, known as turnip greens.

### SOWING

**Sow turnip seeds in cell flats** under cover and once the risk of frost has passed, plant seedlings out in the garden 4in (10cm) apart with 12in (30cm) between rows. Keep them well watered.

**The simplest way to sow** beets is directly into the soil. Its seeds are large and easy to handle. It should be sown directly into furrows 1in (2.5cm) deep and 1½in (4cm) apart. When the seedlings emerge, thin them out to 4in (10cm) apart—save the tender thinnings to use in salads.

### HARVESTING

**Turnips can be lifted** after just five to six weeks as sweet, tender roots; when fully mature at 10 weeks, they make a gourmet treat with their earthy flavors. They can also be treated as cut-and-come-again plants if you harvest the young leaves.

**Harvest beets** gently with a garden fork once they reach the size of a large orange—this will be after about 12–16 weeks. They can be stored in the same way as carrots (see p.182).

**Turnips**

**Beets**

# How to grow **Parsnips**

full sun

light soil

## Equipment

- Parsnip seeds
- Hoe and fork
- Bamboo poles and string
- Gloves
- Watering can

Parsnips are grown in much the same way as carrots and produce long, edible taproots. They take a long time to grow, but are worth the effort because they are one of the few vegetables hardy enough to stay in the ground during the winter. Like carrots, their seeds don't last long, so always check the expiration date on the packet.

### SOWING

**Parsnips like light**, well-drained soil in full sun. The seeds should be sown directly into the soil since they don't transplant well from pots because of their long taproots. Sow the seeds from mid- to late spring, once the risk of a harsh frost is over. Use bamboo poles and string to mark out rows, then create ¾in (2cm) deep furrows. Sow clumps of four to five seeds every 8–12in (20–30cm). The rows should be 12in (30cm) apart.

**As the seedlings emerge**, thin them out, leaving the strongest plant every 8–12in (20–30cm).

### TROUBLESHOOTING

**Look out for carrot rust flies**, which can attack parsnips. Erect an insect-proof mesh barrier that is at least 24in (60cm) high around the plants.

### HARVESTING AND STORING

**It is best** not to harvest your parsnips until they have been hit by the first frost, because this makes them sweeter. Lift them carefully using a fork.

**Parsnips can stay** in the ground for most of the winter. However, if you need to create more space for sowing early-spring vegetables, they can be stored outside in the garden. Dig the parsnips up with a fork, being careful not to damage them, and heel them in elsewhere. To heel, dig a shallow trench, bundle up the parsnips and lay them close together, then cover up with soil. They take up far less space like this, can be dug up when they are needed, and will keep for a few more weeks.

**Careful!** Wear gloves when working with parsnips, because some people develop a rash when their skin comes in contact with the plants.

# Grow Cabbage

Cabbage and their close relatives, such as Brussels sprouts, broccoli, and kale thrive in heavy, rich soils and sunny locations. Cabbage spends a relatively long time in the ground, but its vitamin-rich leaves are well worth the wait. As well as summer and fall varieties, try growing winter and spring types for a year-round crop.

full sun

moist soil

## Equipment

- Cabbage seeds
- Seed flats
- Potting medium
- Dibber
- Watering can
- Bamboo poles
- Twine
- Trowel
- Fork
- Rake
- Insect-proof netting

Seed flats

Insect-proof netting

**Summer and fall cabbage** *18–24 weeks until harvest*

**Sow seeds** *under cover in early to mid-spring*

**Plant out** *in mid- to late spring once frost has passed*

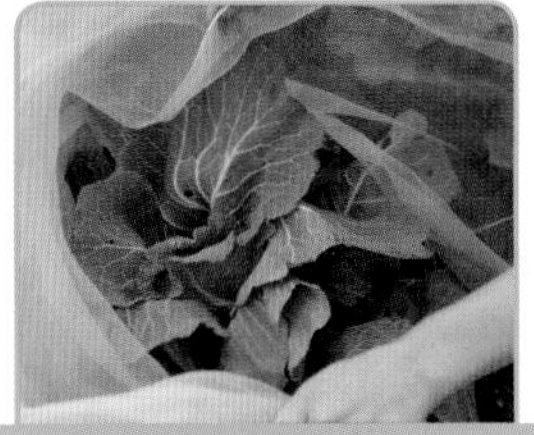

**Protect plants** *from pests using fine, insect-proof netting*

**Harvest** *crops throughout summer and into fall*

**1** Sow cabbage seeds into seed flats or small plastic pots filled with general-purpose potting mix. Using a dibber, make a ½-in (1-cm) hole in each seed flat or pot. Drop two or three seeds in each hole. Cover the seeds with potting mix and water in well.

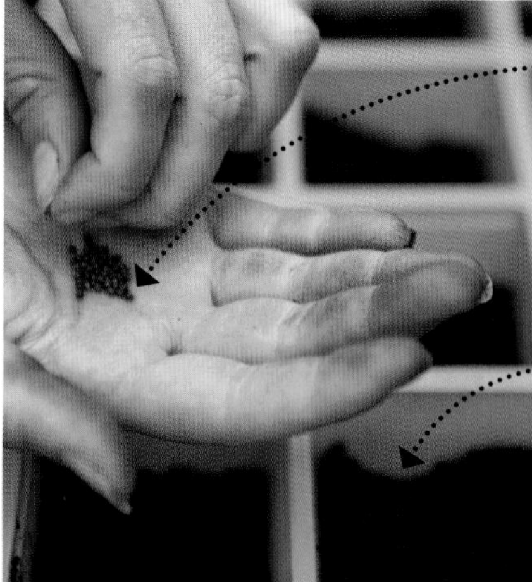

*Tip the seeds into your hand to make it easy to control how many you sow*

*Cabbage are hungry plants, so use high-quality compost*

*When the seedlings look like this, they are ready to be planted out*

**2** The seeds should germinate within about 10 days, depending on the variety and time of year they are sown. Thin the cabbage seedlings so that just the strongest and healthiest plant remains per pot or cell.

**Remember** When the seedlings are about 3in (8cm) tall, they are ready to be planted outside.

**3** Prior to planting out the seedlings, you'll need to thoroughly prepare the soil. Cabbage are hungry plants so will need plenty of manure dug into the soil. Water the seedlings, slide them from their pots, and plant them 16in (40cm) apart.

**Careful!** Ensure that you don't damage the roots when planting out your seedlings.

*Plant cabbage into rich, heavy soil containing well-rotted manure*

*Ensure the base of the stem is level with the soil*

**4** Water the young cabbage well as they start to grow. During hot spells in the summer they may need watering every day. Cabbage plants will also benefit from the occasional liquid fertilizer in summer.

**Careful!** When watering in the summer, avoid splashing the leaves—this can scorch them.

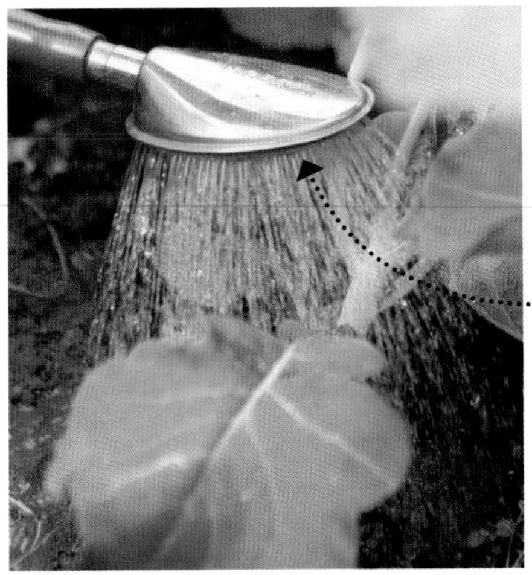

Use a fine nozzle attached to the watering can to distribute the water gently around the plant

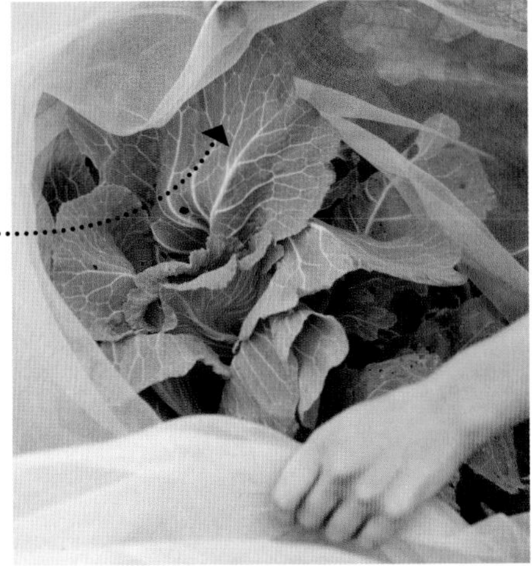

Use a very fine mesh to prevent pests from getting to the plants

**5** Place very fine mesh around the cabbage as they develop throughout the season. This will help keep away the three major pests: cabbage root maggots, birds, and cabbage white caterpillars. Check the plants regularly for infestations.

**Careful!** If you find cabbage white caterpillars, remove the eggs and caterpillars by hand immediately.

**6** Your cabbage will be ready to harvest about 30 weeks after sowing. They should be harvested by cutting through the base of their stem with a knife.

**Tip** Cabbage are large and bulky to store, so harvest the crop as and when needed—cabbage can stay in the garden for a few weeks until needed.

Harvest every other cabbage along the row to allow the rest to continue maturing

# Caring for your **Cabbage**

Cabbage come in a range of colors and shapes and is a very rewarding crop to grow, provided you can keep the heads safe from pests and disease.

The heart is the best part to eat—trim off the tough, outer leaves

To keep your cabbage looking this good, you will need to protect them from pests

Once harvested cabbage can be left to resprout leaves from the stump

## Things to watch out for...

**Garden pests** The worst culprits are birds, which can tear cabbage to shreds, so cover the plants up with a net to keep them safe. Cabbage white butterflies and cabbage root flies are the other pests to watch out for. Netting will deter butterflies, while a cabbage collar (see p.128) will keep cabbage root flies from laying their eggs on or near your plants.

**Clubroot** If seedlings become stunted, wilted, or discolored, it may be a sign of clubroot. This fungal disease causes swellings filled with spores on the roots of plants. The disease can survive in the soil for up to 20 years, so dig up and destroy infected plants and rotate crops in future years.

**Dry soil** Give these hungry plants liquid fertilizer every few weeks as they grow to keep them healthy. Water them daily during periods of drought.

**Seasonal plantings** It is possible to grow a year-round supply of cabbage if you plan carefully. The name of the cabbage indicates when it will be ready to harvest. Spring cabbage are grown over winter and harvested early in the year. They are often grown closely together and harvested as young, tender crops. Summer and fall cabbage are sown in spring and harvested in late summer, and cope well with hot conditions. Winter cabbage are often the ornamental type that can be used in kitchen gardens and bedding designs, and are ready to harvest from late fall onward.

**Also learn to grow ▸▸▸**

# How to grow **Broccoli**

full sun

moist soil

## Equipment

- Broccoli seeds
- Well-rotted manure
- Bamboo poles and string
- Spade
- Rake
- Watering can

Broccoli grows well in many types of soil and is not difficult to cultivate. It prefers a sunny location that drains well. Broccoli is tasty eaten raw in salads or with dips and can be steamed or added to soups or side dishes for color and nutrients.

### PREPARING THE SOIL

**Broccoli should be sown directly** in the soil where it is to be grown. Prepare the soil before planting by digging it over thoroughly and removing any weeds. Add plenty of well-rotted manure or compost to the soil (see p.15).

### SOWING

**Sow the seeds** in mid-spring. Stretch out a string between two poles and create a furrow ½in (1cm) deep. Thinly sow the seeds into the furrow. Carefully push the soil back on top of them and water them in well. Seedlings will appear about 10 days later. As the plants develop, they should be thinned out to a final spacing of 12in (30cm) between each plant.

### CARE

**As the plants grow**, keep the soil free from weeds, which will compete with the seedlings for nutrients, water, and light. Keep the plants well watered to prevent fungal diseases.

### TROUBLESHOOTING

**The main pest to watch out for** on broccoli, and other plants from the brassica family, is the cabbage root fly. It lays its eggs at the base of the plant and the emerging larvae munch on the root system. To protect your plants, place a collar at their base or lay carpet scraps around plants to prevent the eggs from being laid (see p.128). Cover the plants with a net to stop butterflies from laying their eggs nearby and to stop birds from destroying the crop.

### HARVESTING

**Broccoli will be ready** to harvest from midsummer to early fall. Harvest when the flower heads have developed but just before they actually open. Remove them using a sharp knife.

# Grow Beans Up a Tepee

Runner beans are tasty and incredibly productive crops that will continue to produce beans as you harvest them. Training the plants to scramble up a tepee creates an attractive feature in the vegetable garden—these rustic constructions add height and structure, while the brightly colored flowers give them an ornamental quality.

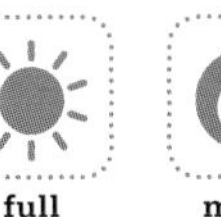

full sun
moist soil

## Equipment

- Bean seeds
- General-purpose potting mix
- Plastic pots
- Large container
  such as a tote, with drainage holes
- 6 bamboo poles
- String
- Crocks or mesh screening
- Watering can

**Bean seeds**

**General-purpose potting mix**

**Crocks**

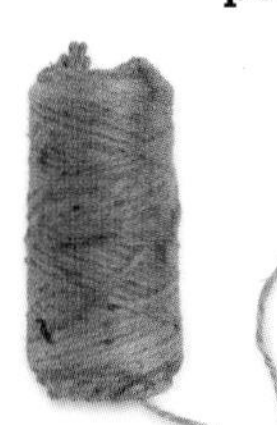

**String**

**Bamboo poles**

**Watering can**

**Plastic pots**

**Large container**

**Runner beans** *12–16 weeks until harvest*

**Sow** *seeds under cover in mid- to late spring*

**Water** *the seedlings well, especially in hot summer weather*

**Harvest** *the pods from midsummer and into fall*

**1** Sow runner bean seeds into small plastic pots in mid- to late spring; sow two seeds per pot. Use high-quality, general purpose potting mix and keep the pots on a sunny windowsill or in a small greenhouse until the risk of cold has passed. Thin out the seedlings after a couple of weeks, leaving the healthiest, strongest plant per pot.

*Seeds can either be sown directly into the soil or put into pots first*

*Create a sturdy structure by winding twine around the poles at 12-in (30-cm) intervals*

*Consider using tree twigs, which can look more attractive and rustic than these bamboo poles*

**2** Place crocks or screening in the bottom of a large container with drainage holes, and then fill with potting mix, adding some general-purpose fertilizer as you go. Insert 6½-ft (2-m) bamboo poles around the edge of your container, about 10in (25cm) apart. Using garden twine, tie together the poles at the top of the tepee, and then secure at regular intervals down the length.

**3** Arrange the plants around the edge of the container, making sure each plant has its own pole. Use a trowel to dig out a hole for each plant, then remove the plants from their pots and place into their holes. Firm them in and water well.

*Cover the plants with soil mix to prevent them from drying out*

**4** As the young plants start to grow, they can be trained up the bamboo poles; twist them around the poles and tie in place. Once they become established, they should begin to use their tendrils to climb on their own.

**Careful!** Monitor the plants for any signs of damage on the leaves, which could be caused by pests such as slugs or blackflies.

*Use twine to begin training plants up the poles*

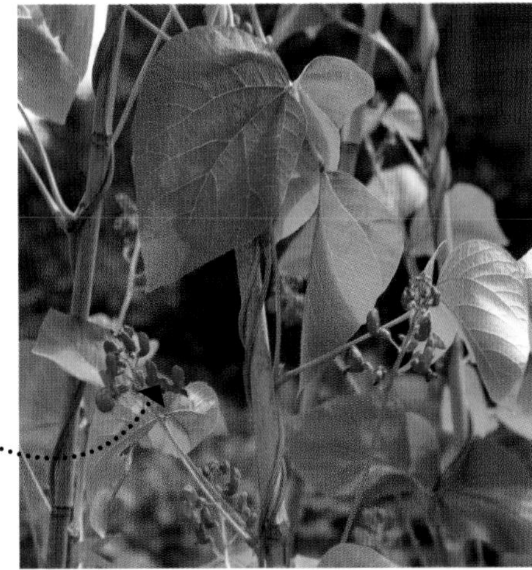

*The pretty flowers not only look good but will also attract bees to your garden*

**5** Keep checking the plants as they grow, because some wayward shoots will need retying and training in. Once the plants reach the top of the tepee, remove the growing tips to stop them from getting any taller.

**Tip** Remove any weeds, water the plants regularly, and give them weekly liquid fertilizer.

**6** It takes about 12 weeks from sowing to harvesting. Pick regularly to keep the plants producing—once they start they will provide a bumper crop over several months; each plant can produce about 2¼lb (1kg) of beans.

**Careful!** Do not leave the ripe beans on the plant too long, or they will become stringy.

*Pick the beans regularly to encourage them to crop longer*

# Caring for your **Runner Beans**

Fresh runner beans are a real treat in summer, and growing them is easy as long as you give them sturdy supports and pick them regularly to keep them cropping.

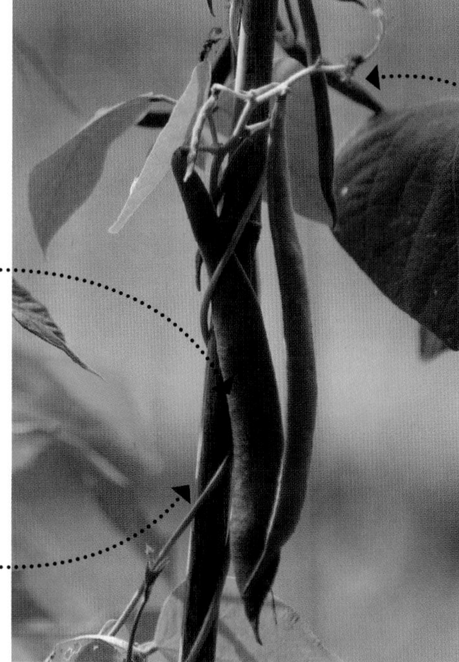

If large bean pods are tough and stringy, remove them and add to the compost heap

Beans are climbing plants so need supporting with stakes

Pick regularly to keep the plant producing beans

## Things to watch out for...

**Wayward plants** Runner beans cling using their twining tendrils and need a good support system to keep them upright. Check that supports are sturdy and that plants are tied in as they grow to keep them neat and tidy. They can easily reach up to 10ft (3m) high, so pinch back the growing tips once they reach the top of their supports to keep them within bounds; smaller dwarf varieties are also available.

**Dry soil** When growing in a pot, runner beans will need watering most days, so keep an eye on the soil to make sure it doesn't dry out. Give the plants a weekly feed with liquid fertilizer.

**Pests** Keep an eye out for slugs and snails, which will munch on the young leaves at seedling stage —see p.67 for tips on how to deal with them. Mice can also dig up and eat seeds just after they have been sown, so protect them with a cloche.

**Poor flowering** Occasionally, beans can fail to set flowers, which means they won't produce a crop. Keeping the plant regularly watered and fed can help to prevent this. Generally, white and pink flowering types will flower more readily than red.

**Stringy pods** Beans need to be picked every few days, otherwise the plant stops producing flowers. Pods that have been left for too long will be stringy and tough and should be thrown away.

**Also learn to grow ▸▸▸**

# How to grow **Peas**

full sun

moist soil

## Equipment

- Pea seeds
- Plastic guttering or plastic pots
- Dibber
- General-purpose potting mix
- Watering can
- Spade
- Rake
- Well-rotted manure
- Pea sticks or pea netting

Peas and beans belong to the same vegetable family, and like very similar growing conditions. Peas can be sown any time from early spring to late summer, and will provide you with a regular supply of pods if you sow them little and often.

### SOWING

**Get your seeds** off to an early start in spring by taking a length of plastic guttering and filling it with general-purpose potting mix. Sow seeds 2in (5cm) apart and 2in (5cm) deep, then cover them up with more mix. Alternatively, sow the seeds in individual pots. Water them well, and leave to germinate in a greenhouse or on a window ledge. Prepare the soil outside by digging it over, removing all weeds, and incorporating some well-rotted manure. When the seedlings have appeared and the soil is warm enough, the plants can be slid out of the guttering into a shallow trench in the soil, or planted out, 2in (5cm) apart.

### CARE

**Peas are climbing plants** and need supports to climb up. Push stakes or twiggy pea sticks into the ground next to the seedlings. Alternatively, stretch pea netting or chicken wire upright next to them.

**Keep the plants** well watered as they grow, particularly when they begin to flower, since they may fail to produce flowers if the soil is dry.

**Cover the plants** with netting since birds love to strip the foliage and pods from the plants.

**Pinch back** the growing tips of the plants once they reach the top of their supports because some varieties can become very tall.

### HARVESTING

**Pea plants can keep producing pods** if they are regularly picked, so keep checking the plants. If you experience a glut, peas can be frozen, and sometimes taste even sweeter after freezing.

# Grow Fall Raspberries

Planting raspberries is a rewarding long-term project. They will be in the ground for about 15 years, so it is important to consider the location very carefully. Growing these plump, mouth-watering berries requires practical skill in building training systems as well as thinking one or two years ahead when it comes to pruning techniques.

full sun

light soil

## Equipment

- Raspberry canes
  - fall-fruiting varieties
- Well-rotted manure
- Fork
- Rake
- Sturdy posts and string or wire
- Trowel
- Watering can
- Pruners
- Gloves
- Plant labels
- General-purpose fertilizer

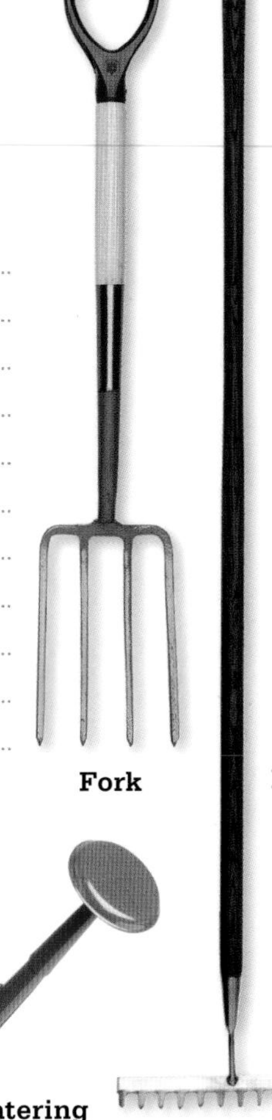
Fork

Posts

Well-rotted manure

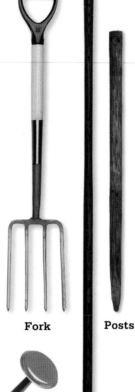

String

General-purpose fertilizer

Pruners

Watering can

Rake

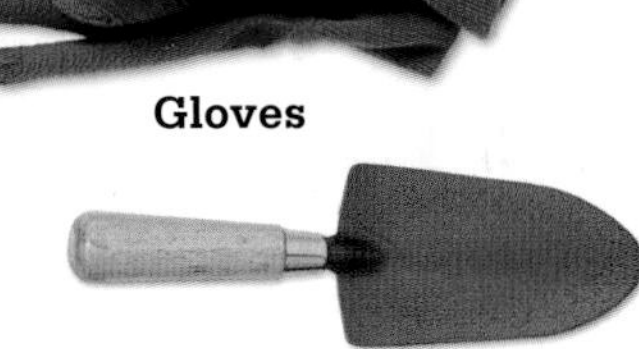
Gloves

Trowel

**Fall raspberries** *6–8 weeks until harvest*

**Plant** *bare-root canes in winter; potted canes any time of year*

**Water** *the canes well, especially in hot summer weather*

**Harvest** *fruit from late summer and into the fall*

**1** Prepare your soil thoroughly and dig it over. Erect a support system by inserting sturdy posts at 3-foot (1-meter) intervals along either side of where you plan to plant your row. Connect the posts with several secure lines of wire or string—you will tie your plants to these wires. Plant the raspberry canes about 16in (40cm) apart between the supports. The canes should be planted shallowly, roughly about 2in (5cm) deep.

Do not plant too deeply or the canes will rot

**2** The leafy green shoots will start to appear in spring. Using pruners, cut the original cane back to the lowest bud or shoot above ground level, being careful not to damage any of the new growth. As the canes grow, they will need to be securely attached to the wires with string.

**Tip** Feed the plants with some general fertilizer and keep them well weeded.

**3** Recently planted canes will need watering about twice a week during the growing season. Raspberries are prone to produce suckers, which are new shoots that emerge from the base of the plant and grow away from the row of plants. Remove these—they will take nutrients and water away from the main plants.

Aim the water at the base of the plant, directly above its root system

**4** Harvest the raspberries when they are plump and juicy. Fall-fruiting raspberry plants should be left in the ground over winter and then pruned the following spring. Cut back all the fruited shoots to ground level.

**Careful!** If you are growing summer-fruiting types as well, keep them clearly separated, since these will need pruning in fall rather than spring.

Always wear gloves when handling the canes

## Caring for your **Raspberries**

Planting fall-fruiting raspberries is easy. Looking after them for the next 15 years is slightly trickier. Make sure you support them well and prune them properly.

Raspberries can also come in yellow and gold colors too

Fall-fruiting varieties are not as vulnerable to attack from birds as summer types

It's best to pick the fruit on a dry day

### Things to watch out for...

**Summer-fruiting varieties** These raspberries fruit in summer and are pruned immediately after harvesting. They are more vigorous than fall-fruiting plants and need a more extensive support system.

**Yellow leaves** Raspberries prefer slightly acidic soil. If the leaves turn yellow, this might be due to lime-induced chlorosis, which is caused by an alkaline soil—it can cause the plant to become deficient in vital nutrients, such as iron and manganese. Acidify the soil using sulfur chips.

**Sagging stems** Make sure you tie in your plants regularly and keep them well supported. Not only will this mean that plants have better airflow between the stems, reducing the chance of disease, but it is also easier to harvest fruit from a neat plant.

# Plant an Apple Tree in a Pot

Growing an apple tree in a pot is ideal if you want your own apples but are short on space. Choose a tree grown on a dwarf rootstock since these trees stay small and compact. A bud from the original variety is grafted onto roots from a less vigorous tree—it is the roots that mainly determine how large the tree will become.

full sun

light soil

## Equipment

- Apple tree on dwarf rootstock such as M26 or MM106
- Large, cold-proof container
- Crocks
- General-purpose potting mix
- Controlled-release fertilizer
- Pole and string
- Watering can
- Liquid fertilizer
- Pruners

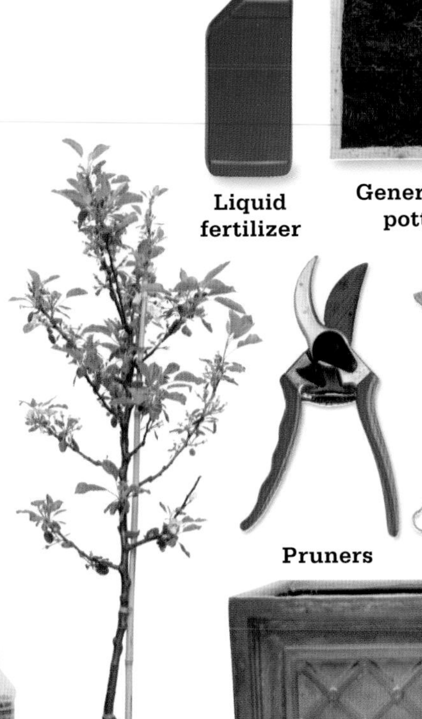
Liquid fertilizer
General-purpose potting mix
Pruners
Crocks
String

Watering can

Controlled-release fertilizer

Apple tree

Container

Pole

**Apples** *14–20 weeks until harvest*

**Plant** *bare-root trees in winter; potted trees all year*

**Water** *the tree well after planting and over the summer*

**Thin** *the fruitlets in midsummer to produce larger crops*

**Harvest** *the fruit from late summer into fall*

**1** Soak the apple tree thoroughly in a bucket of water for a few hours prior to planting. The tree should ideally be grown on a semidwarfing rootstock such as M26 or MM106, so that the tree remains a compact size.

**Tip** It is important that the root ball is allowed to absorb as much water as possible, since it will be harder to thoroughly soak it once it is planted in its container.

*Apple trees produce attractive blossoms as well as delicious fruit*

*Soak the roots of the tree prior to planting*

*Choose a cold-resistant container*

*Covering the drainage holes with crocks prevents the roots from rotting*

**2** Ensure the container for the apple tree is cold-proof. It should be about 16in (40cm) wide and have drainage holes in the bottom. Prepare the container by placing crocks in the bottom to aid drainage.

**Tip** Make sure you have put the container into its final location before weighing it down with potting mix and the plant.

**3** Add a high-quality, general-purpose potting mix into the container. Mix in controlled-release fertilizer as you go—it will supply the plant with essential nutrients when it needs them.

**Careful!** When filling the container, make sure that you leave enough space for the volume of the root ball.

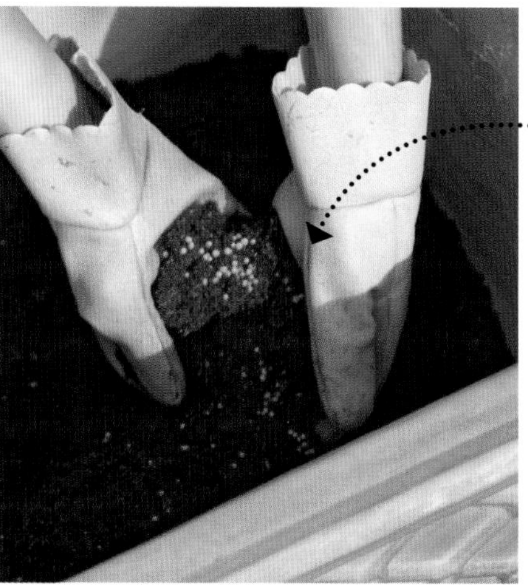

*Wear gloves when handling the fertilizer granules*

**4** Gently remove the tree from the pot and place it in the potting mix, making sure the top of the root ball is just below the rim of the container.

**Tip** Tease out the roots before planting to make sure they spread out and grow strongly into the soil mix, rather than growing inward and strangling the tree.

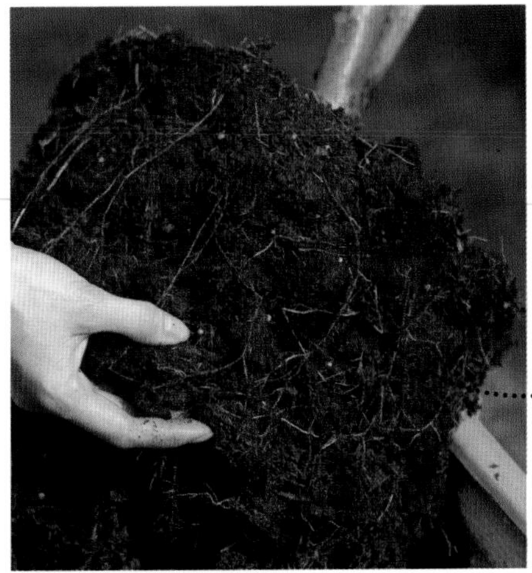

*These fibrous roots should be teased out before planting*

**5** Pack the soil mix around the root ball, ensuring that it is level with the base of the tree trunk, and then water in well. Insert a stake to support and anchor the tree—make sure that it is straight and securely attached with a tree tie. Finally, mulch the surface with pebbles or manure to help suppress weeds and conserve soil moisture.

# Caring for your **Apple Tree**

Apple trees in containers make attractive features for patios and balconies. Techniques such as pruning and thinning the fruit will help the tree to thrive.

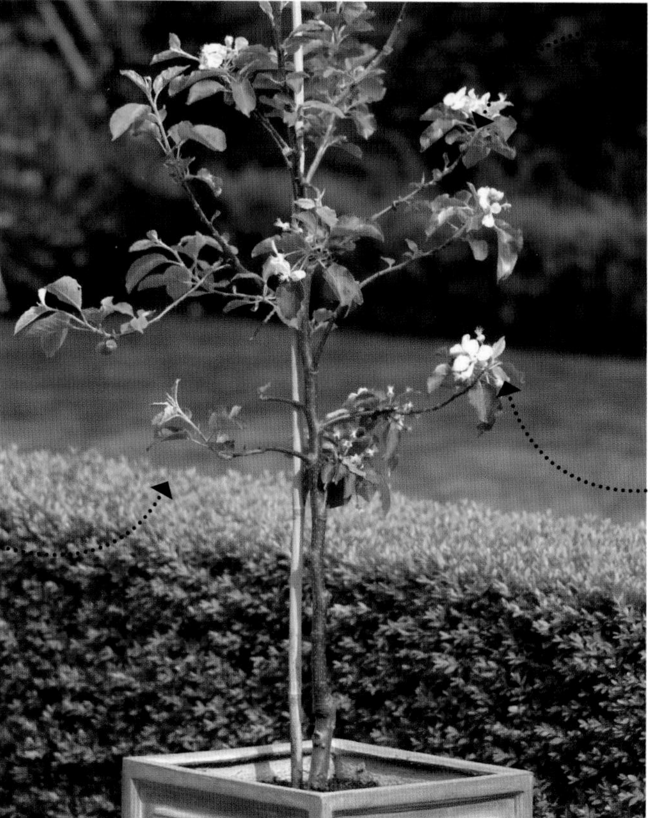

*Look out for diseased or dead wood and cut it out right away*

*Remember to prune the tree each year during winter to stimulate new growth*

*Check the variety of tree since it may need another apple tree nearby to pollinate it*

## Things to watch out for...

**Dry soil** Apple trees grown in containers should be placed in a sheltered location in full sun, which will mean they are prone to drying out. Keep them well watered and give them a liquid feed such as tomato fertilizer once a week during the growing season.

**Birds** Place a net over the apple tree in summer to stop birds from pecking at the fruit.

**Congested branches** Apples trees should have a light prune each winter to remove any crossing or damaged branches.

**An excess of fruit** For the best crops of fruit, apples should be thinned in midsummer—reduce clusters of fruit down to just one or two apples.

**Thickening trunks** Check the tree ties once a year and loosen them slightly if it looks like they might damage the growing trunk.

**Also learn to grow ▸▸▸**

# How to plant a **Fig Tree in a Pot**

full sun

moist soil

## Equipment

- Fig tree
- High-quality, soil-based potting mix
- Cold-resistant container
- Crocks
- Stake and tree tie
- Watering can
- Liquid fertilizer

### SUITABILITY

**Fig trees are easier to grow** than you might think. Despite their associations with the Mediterranean, the trees are very hardy and can tolerate low temperatures. The difficulty is getting them to fruit, since this requires sunshine and warmth. Figs are well suited to growing in a pot. In fact, they will produce more fruit if their roots are restricted than if planted in the bed or border. The restriction forces the plant to reproduce by developing fruit rather than growing a lot of leafy growth.

### PLANTING

**Figs should be planted** in cold-resistant containers with a diameter of about 16in (40cm). Ensure the container has drainage holes and place crocks over them. Plant trees into free-draining, soil-based potting mix and water them in well.

### CARE

**Fig trees will need watering daily** during the summer months since the container will drain quickly. They will fruit better if given liquid fertilizer weekly and benefit from a compost mulch each spring. Figs should be repotted into fresh soil mix every few years, but do not give them a larger pot because they fruit best with restricted roots.

### FRUITING

**Fruit is produced** at the tips of the shoots. In cooler climates, figs only produce one crop of fruit a year, which is formed from fruitlets that overwinter and mature the following summer. Remove any newly formed fruit at the end of summer—it will not survive the winter. Protect the fruit from birds and wasps using netting.

### PRUNING

**Minimal pruning is required** on a fig tree. Occasionally older wood should be removed in winter, with younger wood left as a replacement. Pinch off growing tips in spring to encourage the formation of more fruitlets, and trim back any leaves that shade the swelling fruit in summer.

# Plant Black Currants

The jet-black berries dangling from the branches of a black currant bush make a great addition to any kitchen garden. Black currants are grown as stool bushes, which means they are planted deep into the soil and their shoots emerge straight from the ground.

full sun

moist soil

Plant labels

## Equipment

- Black currant plant
- Fork
- Rake
- Spade
- Well-rotted manure
- Poles and string
- Controlled-release fertilizer
- Watering can
- Plant labels

Watering can

Controlled-release fertilizer

Well-rotted manure

Fork

Spade

Rake

String

Bamboo poles

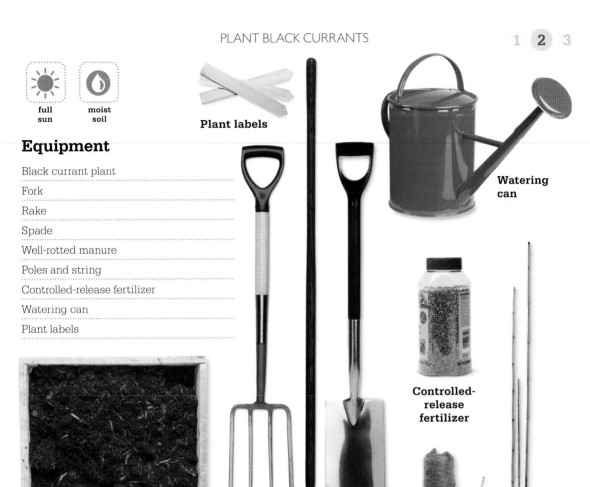

**Black currants** *10–12 weeks until harvest*

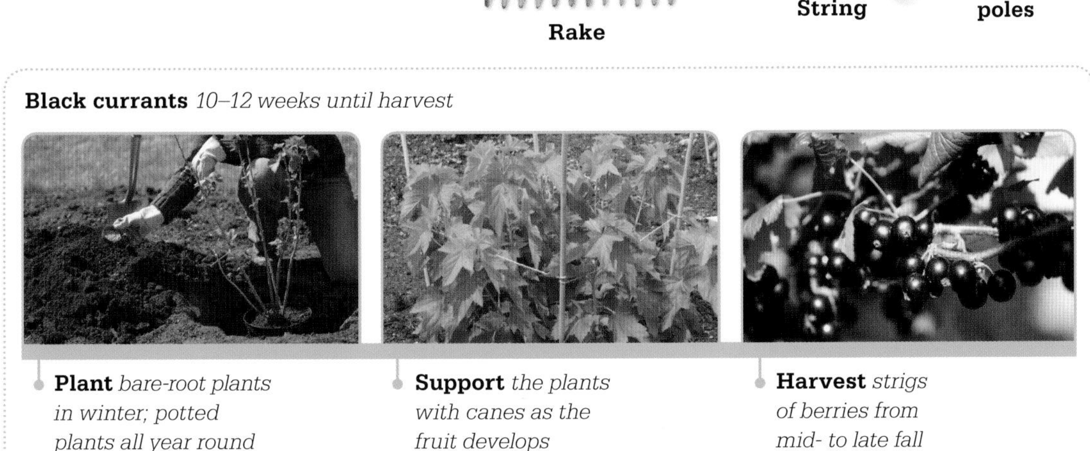

**Plant** *bare-root plants in winter; potted plants all year round*

**Support** *the plants with canes as the fruit develops*

**Harvest** *strigs of berries from mid- to late fall*

**1** Dig a hole double the width of the black currant plant's root ball and about 4in (10cm) deeper than the depth of the pot. Use a bamboo pole placed across the hole to check the depth against the plant's stem—the plant needs to be slightly deeper in the ground than in its pot. Add potting mix or well-rotted manure to the soil from the hole. Use this mix to backfill around the root ball.

*Firm in close to the stem, but be careful not to damage it*

**2** Firm the plant in using your hands or feet, and then rake the ground level afterward. Give the plant a thorough soaking using a watering can with a fine nozzle attachment. Sprinkle a general-purpose fertilizer around the root area and mulch with well-rotted manure.

**Tip** If you are planting more than one, space them 5ft (1.5m) apart.

**3** As the plant grows, it will need to be kept well watered, especially during its first summer, and it will also need regular fertilizing. Pull out weeds by hand rather than using a hoe, since this could damage the roots. Apply a mulch of manure in spring.

**Careful!** The flowers may need protection with garden fabric in spring, if frost is forecast.

*A liquid fertilizer will keep the leaves looking green and healthy*

*A generous dollop of manure around the plant will prevent weeds from germinating*

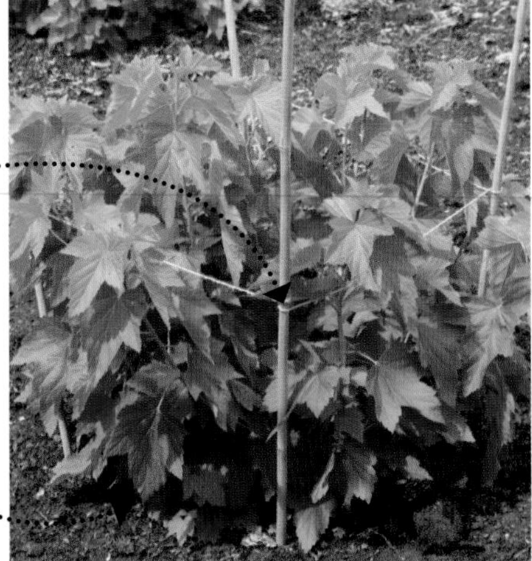

Support the branches with poles and string to prevent branches from snapping


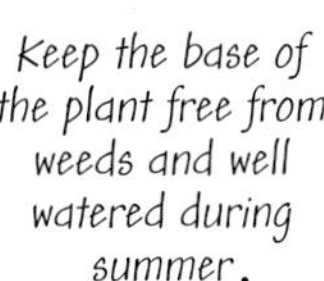

Keep the base of the plant free from weeds and well watered during summer


**4** When the plants start to produce fruit, the branches will need support to prevent them from snapping under the weight. The easiest method is to make a frame: insert four bamboo poles around the plant and tie them together with string.

**Careful!** Place a net over the plants as the fruit ripens to stop birds from devouring the crop.

## Caring for your **Black currants**

Black currants look just as dramatic and impressive as any display of flowers, but are also attractive to birds, so make sure you protect them with netting.

Black currants are easy to grow, but the tiny berries can be tricky to pick
Black currants are a healthy snack and are packed full of vitamin C


### Things to watch out for...

**Ripe berries** These are irresistible to birds, so use netting to protect them. Picking the tiny berries can be difficult because they are so small, so use scissors to cut whole strigs (lengths of stems), once the fruits have turned black.

**Weak growth** Black currants need a heavy, fertile soil with a high nitrogen content to encourage lots of new shoots to emerge each year from the base of the bush. Each spring, apply a fertilizer such as sulfate of ammonia before mulching heavily around the root system. Water the plants well.

**Spindly, congested stems** Black currants should be pruned each year during winter by removing about a third of the old, spindly wood from the base of the plant.

**Also learn to grow ▸▸▸**

# Plant **White and Red currants**

full sun or part shade

light soil

## Equipment

- A white or red currant bush
- Well-rotted manure or compost
- Spade
- Bamboo poles and string
- Pruners
- Netting

White and red currants are the same plant, simply producing different colored fruit. They can be grown equally well in shade or sun, which makes them ideal for growing in north-facing gardens and patios, where other crops may struggle.

### PLANTING

**Currants should be planted** in fall when the ground is still warm. They need fertile soil that has been enriched with well-rotted manure or compost. Plant them so that they sit at the same height in the ground as they did in their pot. Use netting to protect the juicy fruits from birds.

### PRUNING

**Plants should be grown** as an open-centered bush on a small stem about 8in (20cm) off the ground. The center of the canopy should be free from branches, and four or five branches should form the main structure of the bush, making a goblet shape. Currants can also be grown as vertical cordons (see pp.180–181).

**Prune the currants in winter**, ensuring that no new shoots are growing across the center of the plant and that diseased wood is removed. In summer, prune back the new growth to five leaves to allow better air circulation and so that sunlight can reach the fruit (see pp.176–179).

**Whitecurrants**

**Red currants**

# Plant **Gooseberries**

full sun or part shade

light soil

## Equipment

- A gooseberry bush
- Well-rotted manure or compost
- Spade
- Bamboo poles and string
- Pruners
- Netting
- Posts and wires

Gooseberries grow in exactly the same way as white and red currants, and so their treatment is the same too. They should also be pruned in the same way as currants, since they fruit on old wood and the base of new wood. They tolerate shade, so can be planted in north-facing gardens.

### PLANTING

**The plants can be grown** as freestanding bushes and should be spaced 3ft (1m) apart. Alternatively, they can be trained. Before planting, erect a training system of three horizontal wires, placed parallel and stretched between thick posts. Dig a hole that matches the depth of the plant in its container. Place the plant in the hole, firm it down, and water in well. For cordons (see p.180), plant 14in (35cm) apart and attach to vertical bamboo poles tied to the wires.

### PRUNING CORDONS

**Prune bushes** as for currants (see facing page). Remove any crossing, diseased, or damaged wood. Prune cordons twice a year. In summer, the new growth should be cut back to five leaves from the stem. In winter, cut back the new growth to two buds. Do not prune the uppermost shoot, instead train it up the pole until it has reached the top wire.

### CARE

**Keep gooseberries well watered** in their first year, and fertilize and mulch them every following year in spring. As the fruit starts to ripen, net the plants to prevent bird damage.

### TROUBLESHOOTING

**Look out for the hairy caterpillars** of gooseberry sawflies, which can strip the leaves from a plant within days. Remove the caterpillars by hand as soon as you spot them. Gooseberries are susceptible to mildew, so choose resistant varieties such as 'Invicta' and keep the plant regularly watered (see p.66).

# How to **Protect Plants from Pests**

There are simple ways to guard your plants from pests, and many do not require expensive or specialty equipment—you can make them at home from recycled materials. The most important defense is to know your enemies so that you understand the best ways to deter them.

## Netting

Common garden pests, such as birds, mice, and squirrels often strike when the crops are ready for harvesting and at their tastiest, but they can be deterred using netting. Hang the netting from stakes to keep it off the plants and make sure there are no holes or gaps since the pests will quickly find them. Stake the nets to the ground to make them completely secure. Some crops, such as cabbage, should be covered with very fine netting or fabric, which will keep out cabbage white butterflies.

## Cabbage Collars

Cabbage root maggots are a common pest for brassicas such as cabbage and will attack the roots of the plants and cause them to die. There is no effective insecticide so the best defense is a cabbage collar, since placing a barrier around the base of the stems stops the cabbage root flies from landing and laying its eggs. Collars can be bought from local garden centers or you can make your own. Cardboard discs or squares of carpet can be used and are just as effective.

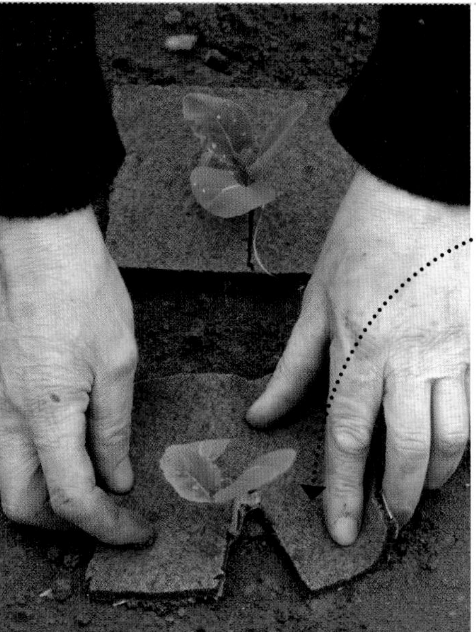

Cut a slit in the square so that it can be positioned without damaging the seedling

Recycle old foil or shiny wrapping paper as a free bird deterrent

## Shiny objects

A simple method of deterring birds from attacking fruit and vegetables is to hang shiny objects nearby that will sway in the wind and shimmer in the sunlight—the flashing light will scare off the birds. Hang old CDs, strips of foil, or shiny paper from pieces of string suspended around your yard.

## Manufactured structures

It is possible to buy manufactured structures that can be placed over individual plants. The beauty of these structures is that they are quick to use and can be stacked easily for storage in the shed. In winter and spring they can be used as cloches for cold protection by wrapping bubble plastic around them. You can even make these yourself from chicken wire.

These structures will protect crops from bird damage

## Fabric

Birds are not the only pests to fly around the veg patch. Carrot rust flies are a major problem too. Larvae tunnel their way through the crops, making them inedible. One method of deterring them is to erect very fine-weave fabric around your plants. Make sure the barrier is at least 24in (60cm) high and secure at the bottom, because the carrot rust flies can't fly high enough to get over this barrier.

# 3

# Take It Further

This final chapter will introduce you to a new range of delicious—often gourmet—crops, including tender asparagus, shiny eggplant, juicy plums, and jewel-like blueberries. Some of these crops require special care and attention, while others are perennial, and will reward the long-term investment of your time and space. But they are all worth the extra effort, and are a great addition to any kitchen garden.

**In this section learn to grow:**

**Leeks**
*see pp.138–143*

**Eggplant**
*see pp.144–149*

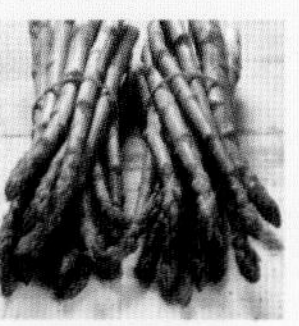

**Asparagus**
*see pp.150–153*

**Artichokes**
*see pp.154–157*

**Herbs**
*see pp.158–163*

**Blueberries**
*see pp.164–167*

**Plums**
*see pp.170–174*

**Storage**
*see pp.182–185*

# Planning a Kitchen Garden

Careful planning is essential for a kitchen garden. In restricted spaces, keep it simple and manageable—choose small amounts of a wider range of crops and only choose crops that you really enjoy eating. The plot plans given here are based on a 10x10ft (3x3m) square plot, but if your space is not this size or shape, take inspiration from these plans and adapt them for your own garden.

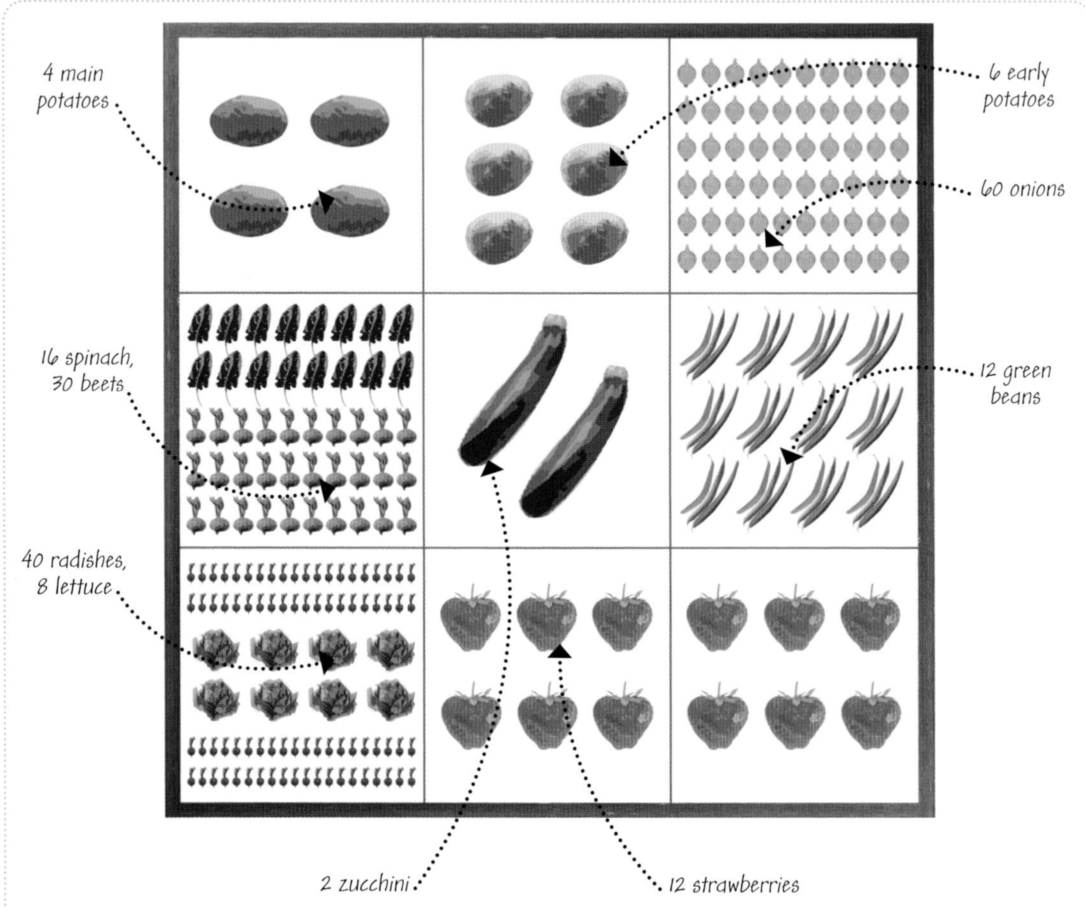


## The easy-to-grow plot

This simple planting plan provides the staple crops of potatoes, onions, and beans along with delicious, quick-growing salad crops such as radishes, beets, and lettuce. Reliable zucchini and spinach plants will produce exciting options for stir-fries, and strawberries will provide a delicious treat in early to midsummer. All these crops are easy to grow and are an excellent starting point if you are planning a vegetable plot for the first time. Position the crops that you will harvest first—here the salad crops—on the outside edge of the space, so that they are easy to reach without disturbing the other crops.

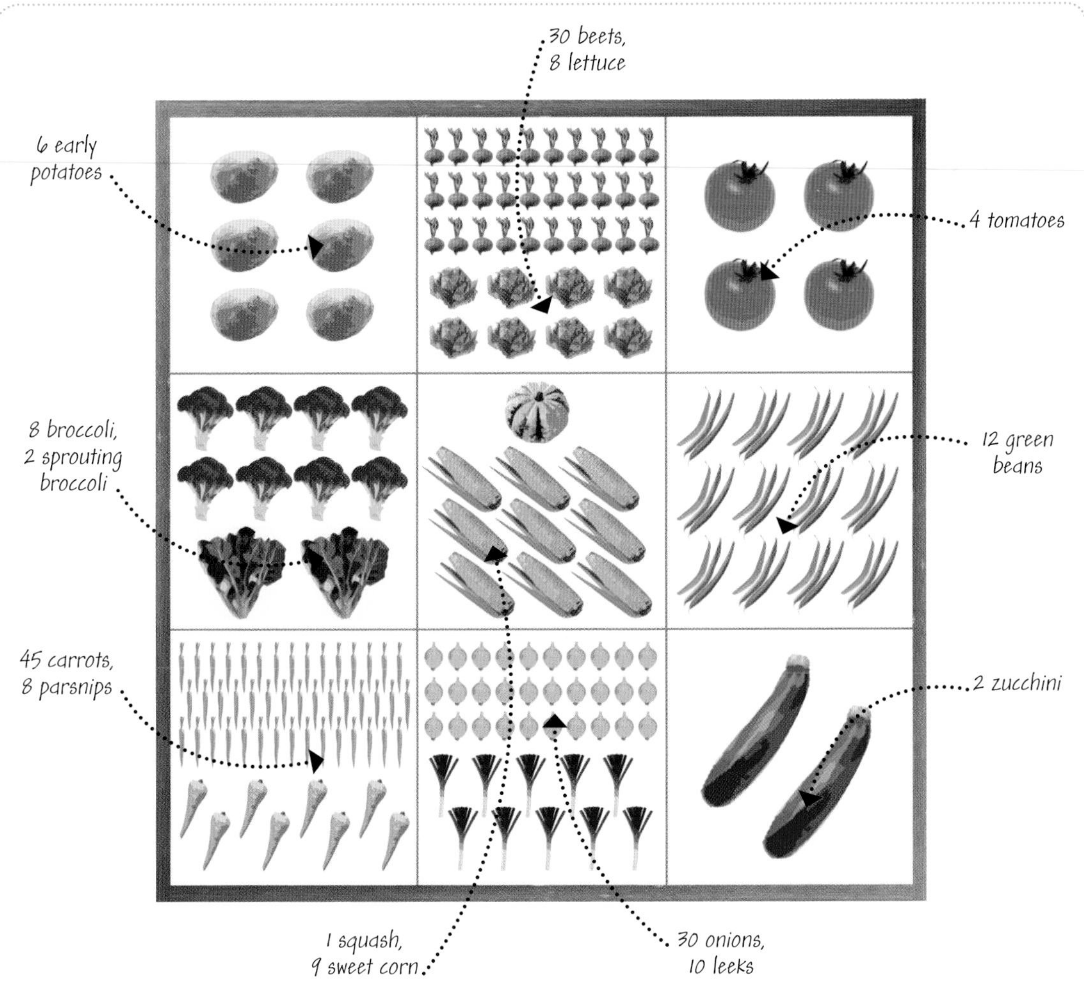


## The family plot

If you want to be adventurous and are trying to expand the list of vegetables your family eats, try this planting combination. This plot is designed for maximum productivity in a small space: a squash is planted low to the ground underneath the tall sweet corn plants; it thrives in this environment, allowing you to maximize your growing space. Some of the crops in this plan are simple to grow, such as the lettuce and tomatoes, while others, such as the sweet corn are more difficult, making this an ideal plot for the family to grow together. Onions, tomatoes, and carrots are probably the most popular ingredients for family meals, and this plan will provide you with plenty, while the two zucchini plants will supply an abundance of vegetables for more exciting recipes. Winter crops such as the broccoli, leeks, parsnips, and purple-sprouting broccoli will provide food later in the season, after most other crops have been harvested. If you want to grow some sweet treats for summer desserts, add strawberries or red currants to this combination.

# Crop Rotation

To avoid a buildup of crop-specific pests and diseases in the soil and to prevent a depletion of certain nutrients, it is important to grow groups of annual crops in different parts of the vegetable patch in subsequent years. Certain types of crops have similar needs and can be grouped together into three distinct "years," although some people choose to create five rotations.

**Beets**

**Carrots**

**Potatoes**

**Radishes**

## Year 1: root vegetables

The root vegetable group includes potatoes, beets, carrots, leeks, lettuce, radishes, onions, parsnips, and spinach. Grow these in the beds after harvesting and clearing the brassica family of vegetables. These crops do not have a very high requirement for nitrogen, so are ideal to follow the brassicas, which will have depleted some of the nitrogen from the soil. The following year, replace the root family with peas, beans, and fruiting vegetables.

Beans

Tomatoes

## Year 2: peas and beans

Peas, beans, and fruiting vegetables are usually planted in the space where the root family grew the year before. This group also includes eggplant, celery, zucchini, pumpkins, sweet corn, chiles, and tomatoes. Peas and beans absorb nitrogen from the air and fix it in the soil, creating a rich environment that benefits the crops that will occupy the space the following year: nitrogen-hungry brassicas will replace them.

Cauliflower

Cabbage

## Year 3: cabbage family

Often referred to as brassicas, this group includes broccoli, purple-sprouting broccoli, cauliflower, Brussels sprouts, kale, rutabagas, and turnips. These crops need a nitrogen-rich site so should be planted into soil vacated by the peas and beans. It is particularly important to move this group of crops around, because they are very susceptible to soil-borne diseases such as clubroot, for which there is no cure and can remain in the soil for years.

# How to make **Compost and Leaf Mold**

A compost bin is useful if you plan on growing more than just a few vegetables in pots. Compost bins don't need much space and can easily be tucked into a corner of your plot. Alternatively, consider making leaf mold, which can be added to the soil to improve its structure.

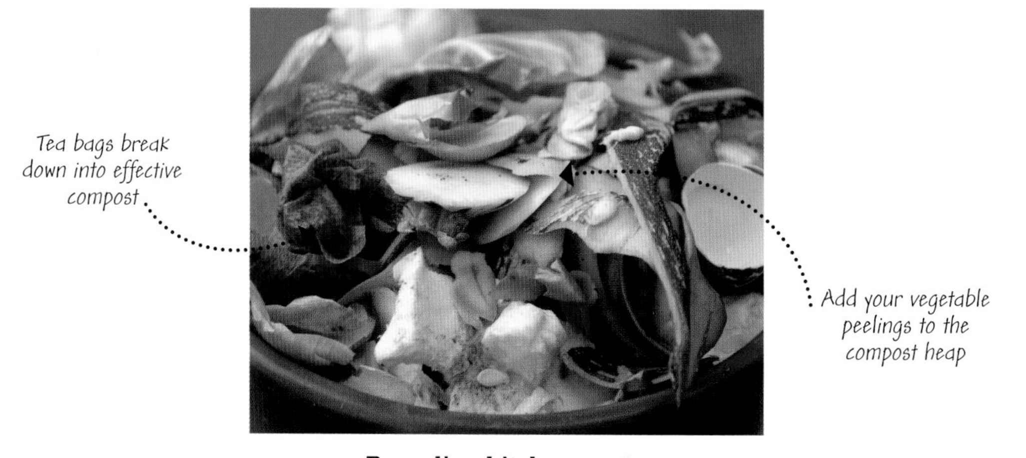

Tea bags break down into effective compost
Add your vegetable peelings to the compost heap


**Recycling kitchen waste**

**Filling up the compost bin**

**Turning the compost**

## Composting

A compost heap should be a mix of carbon-based material, such as shredded newspaper and wood chips, and nitrogen-based matter, such as kitchen waste, which prevents the compost from turning smelly and slimy. Keep the compost heap warm by leaving a lid on it—you can make one from cardboard if you need to—and turn it every few weeks. In two to three months the mixture will have broken down into rich, sweet-smelling compost.

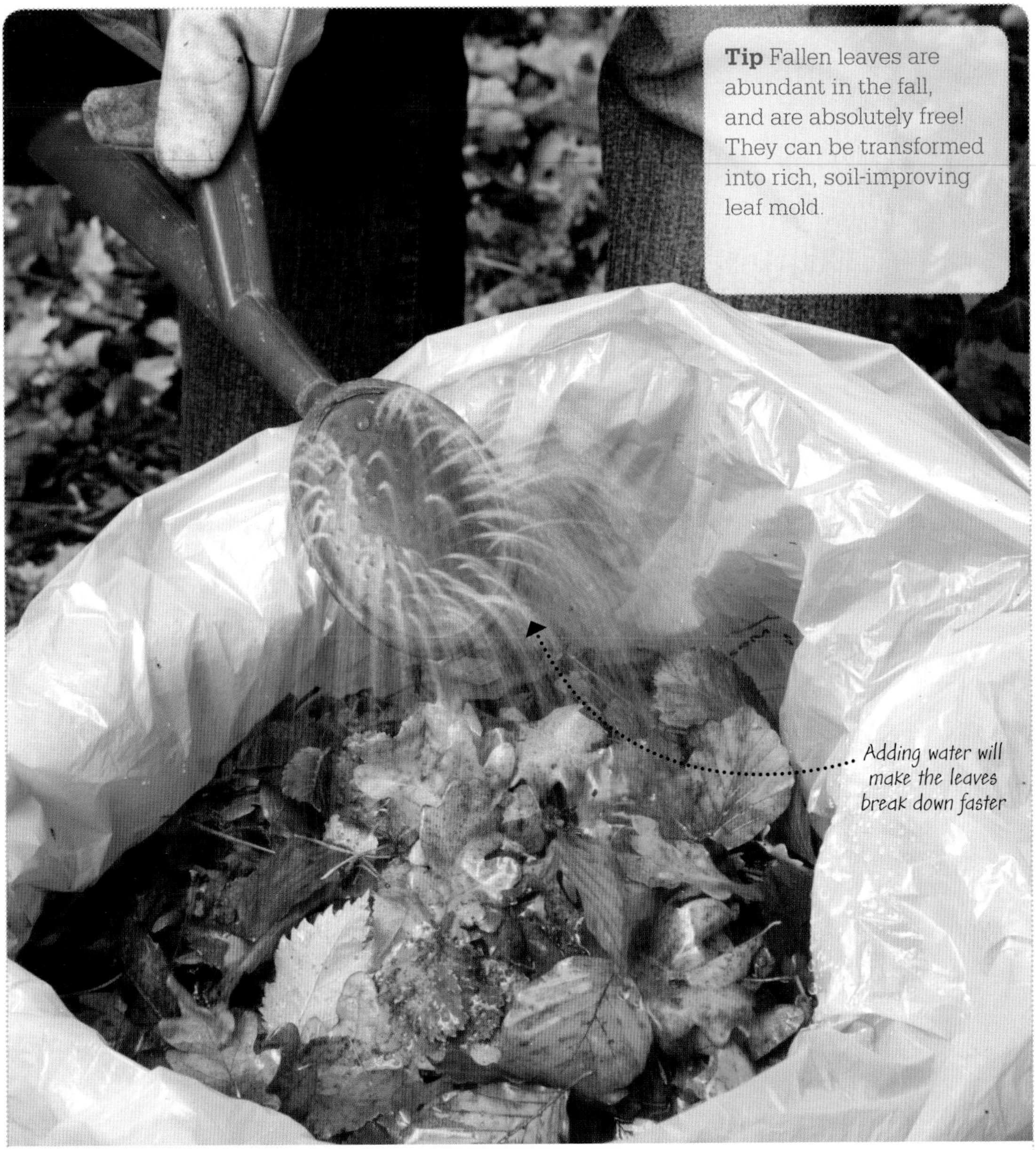

**Tip** Fallen leaves are abundant in the fall, and are absolutely free! They can be transformed into rich, soil-improving leaf mold.

Adding water will make the leaves break down faster

## Making leaf mold

Leaf mold usually has fewer nutrients than compost, but is fantastic for improving soil structure. Rake up leaves in fall and place them in a bin liner. Alternatively, use a rotary mower to gather them up off the lawn, since shredded leaves will break down faster. If the leaves are dry, add water to speed up decomposition. Store them in a cool, dry place and shake up the bag occasionally. The process takes about two years.

# Grow Leeks

With their delicious mild onion flavor, leeks are one of the stalwarts of the winter vegetable garden. They provide a good alternative to cabbage when there is little else available to harvest, and they can be pulled young, to produce tender "baby" leeks.

full sun

light soil

## Equipment

- Leek seeds
- Potting mix
- Trowel
- Biodegradable cell packs
- Watering can
- Hand fork
- Scissors
- Fork and rake
- Well-rotted manure
- Dibber
- Liquid fertilizer

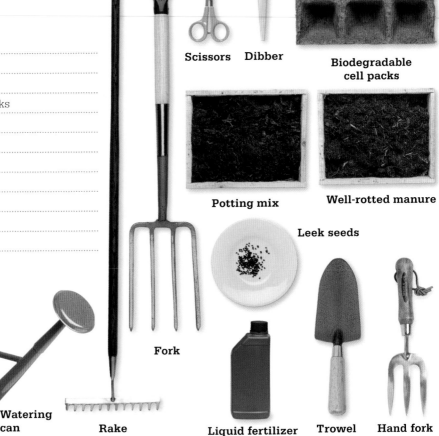

Scissors

Dibber

Biodegradable cell packs

Potting mix

Well-rotted manure

Leek seeds

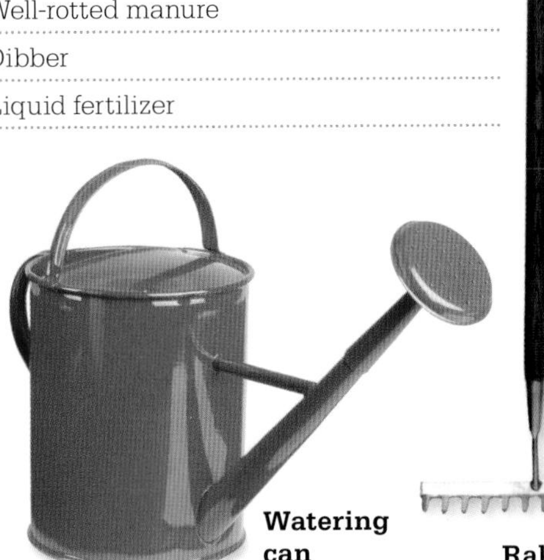

Watering can

Fork

Rake

Liquid fertilizer

Trowel

Hand fork

**Leeks** *30–32 weeks until harvest*

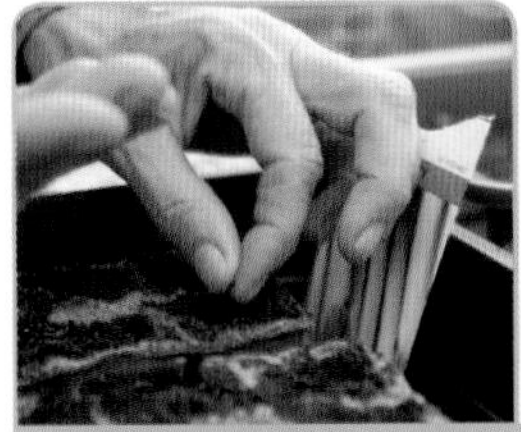

**Sow seed** *in early to mid-spring and keep warm under cover*

**Plant out** *seedlings in late spring to early summer*

**Hill up** *the stems as they grow to block out the light*

**Harvest** *from late summer through to wintertime*

**1** Leeks can be sown under cover in midwinter into biodegradable seed flats or pots filled with seed-starting mix. They must be watered in well and will need to be kept at a temperature of about 50°F (10°C), otherwise they will not germinate.

**Tip** Biodegradable pots allow you to plant out the seedlings without disturbing their root systems.

*Sow three or four seeds into each cell.*

*Check the leeks have an established root system before planting*

**2** Once the seedlings are large enough and the weather has warmed up in late spring, plant them outside into a sheltered seed bed—a temporary outdoor growing location—to allow them to develop into bigger plants.

**Tip** Water the seedlings in well to encourage them to develop fully.

**3** When the seedlings have grown about 10in (25cm) tall they can be planted out into their final growing location. Use a hand fork to gently lift them out of the soil, being careful not to break their delicate leaves or roots.

**Remember** Dig over the vegetable bed and add plenty of well-rotted manure before you transfer your leek plants.

*Lift seedlings ready to be planted in their final location*

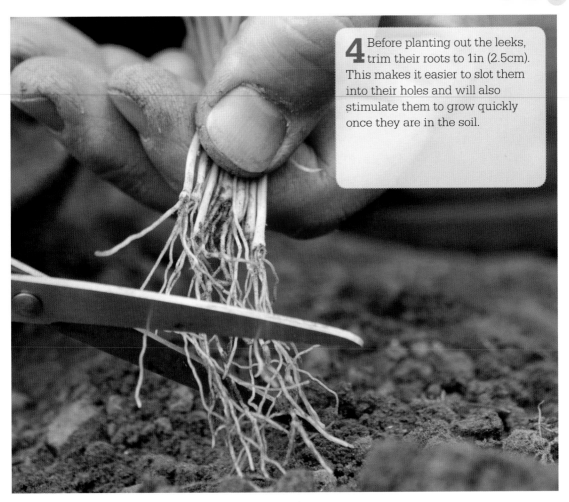

**4** Before planting out the leeks, trim their roots to 1in (2.5cm). This makes it easier to slot them into their holes and will also stimulate them to grow quickly once they are in the soil.

**5** Use a large dibber to create planting holes about 1in (2.5cm) wide, 6in (15cm) deep, and 10in (25cm) apart. Drop the leeks into them so that just their tips stick out of the top.

**Tip** If you want to grow "baby" leeks, which are harvested when they are still small and tender, space seedlings 4in (10cm) apart.

Place the leek seedlings into their holes but do not firm back the soil
These roots still need to be trimmed before planting

**6** Do not push the soil back around the seedlings but instead water them in thoroughly, allowing the soil to loosely crumble around the stems of the leeks. The plants must be kept well watered while the stems are swelling.

**Why?** Leaving space around the seedlings allows their stems to swell easily as they grow.

There should be space around the seedlings
Allow the water to pool a little around the seedling

**7** As the leeks grow, regularly push the soil up around the base of the stems with a trowel. This process, known as blanching, blocks out the light and helps to keep the plants white and tender, as well as making them more stable. Once the leeks are fully grown, harvest them using a fork.

# Caring for your **Leeks**

Leeks are related to the onion family, but rather than producing bulbs, they form tender white stems. Hill up the plants and water regularly to encourage a healthy crop.

*Use leeks as soon as possible after harvesting*

*Leeks are needed winter crops when there is not much else available.*

*Leeks can stay in the ground all winter, so only harvest when needed.*

## Things to watch out for...

**Leek moths and onion flies** The caterpillars of leek moths bore into the leaves and stems of plants, while onion flies attack the roots, causing plants to rot. Remove and destroy any infected plants. Don't be discouraged though, covering the plants with insect-proof mesh will help to deter these pests. Leek rust is another common problem, but resistant varieties are available.

**Weeds** Regularly hoe around the plants to prevent the growth of weeds, which compete for nutrients and can affect the size of your crop.

**Extra space** Leeks can remain in the ground for most of the winter, until you are ready to harvest them, but if you need to use their growing space for other crops, they can be lifted and "heeled in" elsewhere: dig them up and place them in a new hole with fresh soil around their roots.

# Grow Eggplant

Eggplant traditionally needed a warm, sunny, sheltered site or a greenhouse in order to produce fully ripe fruit. However, with the introduction of modern hybrids and grafted varieties, these fascinating plants can now be grown outdoors even in cooler climates.

full sun

moist soil

## Equipment

- Eggplant seeds
- Plastic pots—small and large
- Compost
- Watering can
- Fork
- General-purpose potting mix
- Bamboo poles and string
- Liquid fertilizer
- Plant labels
- Trowel

**Eggplant seeds**

**General-purpose potting mix**

**Trowel**

**Compost**

**Plant labels**

**Plastic pots**

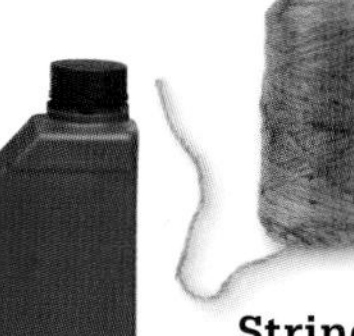
**String**

**Liquid fertilizer**

**Bamboo poles**

**Watering can**

**Fork**

**Eggplant** *24–28 weeks until harvest*

**Sow seeds** *under cover in early spring and keep them warm*

**Plant out** *in late spring once all frost has passed*

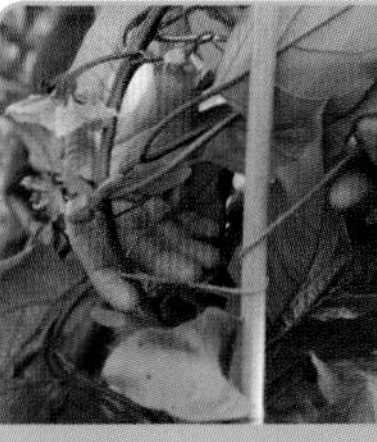
**Support** *the plants as the fruit develop and become heavy*

**Harvest** *the eggplant from late summer into fall*

**1** Fill small plastic pots or plastic cell flats with seed-starting mix in early spring. Firm the soil down and lightly water prior to sowing the seeds.

**Tip** Although eggplant can be bought as young plants in spring, it is cheaper to grow them from seed and start them off indoors.

Press seed mix down into the pot

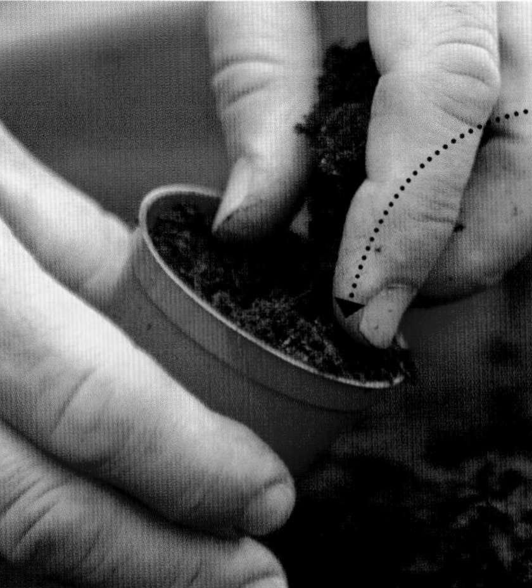

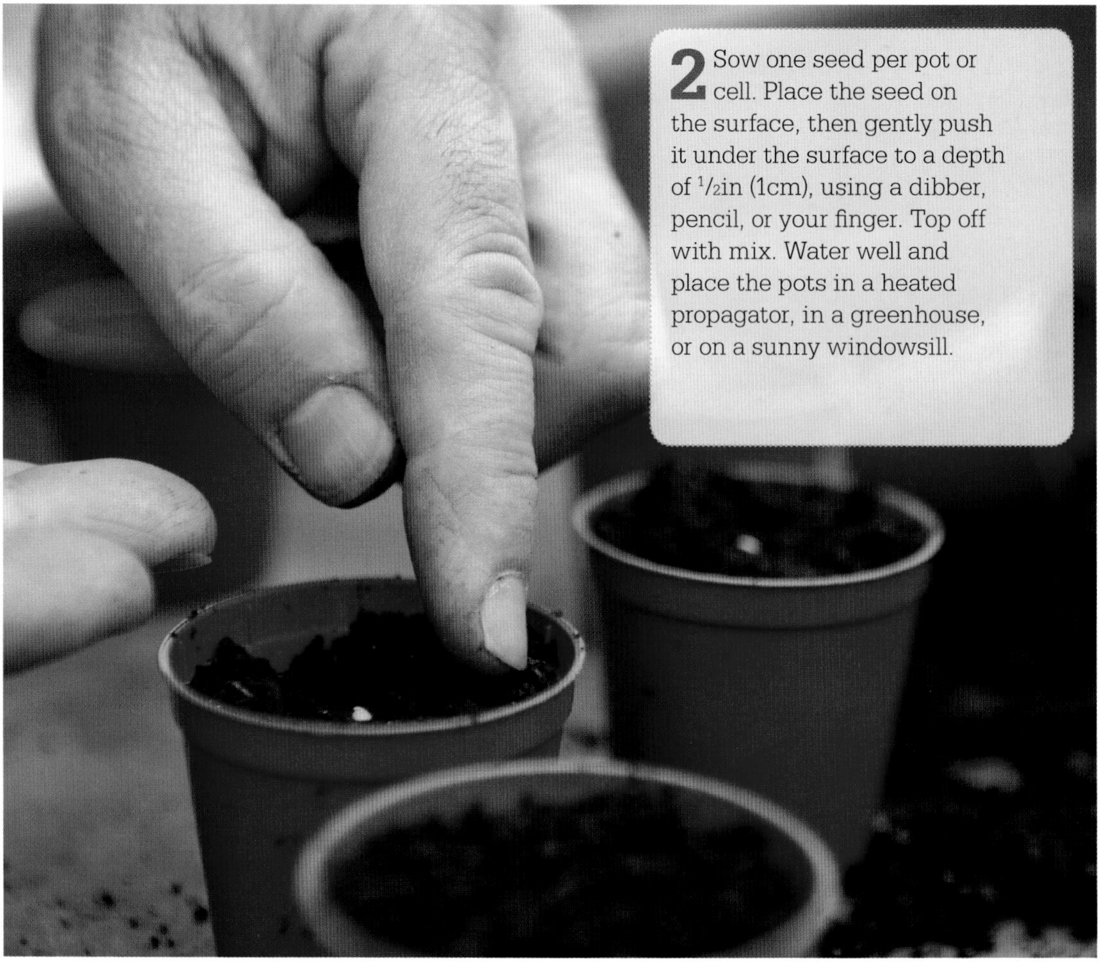

**2** Sow one seed per pot or cell. Place the seed on the surface, then gently push it under the surface to a depth of $^1/_2$in (1cm), using a dibber, pencil, or your finger. Top off with mix. Water well and place the pots in a heated propagator, in a greenhouse, or on a sunny windowsill.

**3** Seeds should start to germinate in about seven to ten days. Once the seedlings are about 2½in (6cm) tall, remove them from the propagator and leave them in the greenhouse or on a windowsill until they are ready to be repotted.

**Remember** Keep checking on the plant to make sure that it hasn't grown too big for its pot, and regularly water it.

*Take the seedlings out of the propagator when they are this height*

*Keep checking the moisture of the soil and add water if it feels dry*

*Push the smaller pot into the larger one to create a planting hole for the seedling*

**4** When roots appear through the drainage holes in the bottom of the pot, it is time to plant it into a bigger container. Plant into 12-in (30-cm) wide pots filled with all-purpose potting mix.

**Tip** If you are growing the plants in a greenhouse, this larger pot will be their final location.

**5** Once the risk of late frost has passed, the plants can be planted out. Harden them off and plant them in a warm, sheltered location in well-prepared soil. Give them a spacing of between 24–30in (60–75cm).

**Remember** Prior to planting out, harden the eggplant off on a porch or in a cold frame (see p.74).

*This plant has an established root system and is ready for planting out*

*Support the plants with stakes and garden twine as they grow*

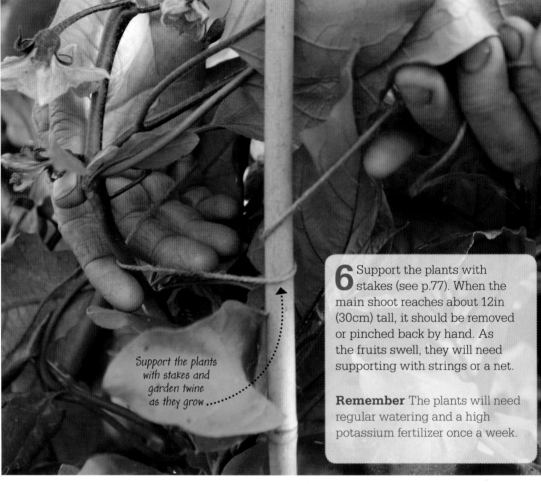

**6** Support the plants with stakes (see p.77). When the main shoot reaches about 12in (30cm) tall, it should be removed or pinched back by hand. As the fruits swell, they will need supporting with strings or a net.

**Remember** The plants will need regular watering and a high potassium fertilizer once a week.

**7** The stems can be tough and woody, so harvest the eggplant by cutting them from the plant with pruners. Regular cutting will encourage further fruiting. Use eggplant quickly—they don't keep well.

**Careful!** Don't leave the fruit on the plant for too long or the skin can turn dull and quickly overripen. Harvest when shiny.

*Ensure that pruners are sharp for a clean cut*

*The fruit here is healthy and shiny and ready for harvesting*

# Caring for your **Eggplant**

Eggplant are trickier to grow than many crops, but are well worth the effort—if you keep them healthy, they can reward you with four to six fruits per plant.

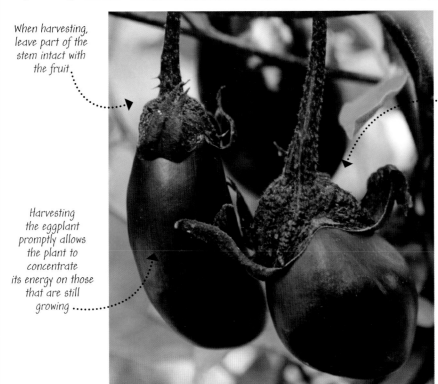

*When harvesting, leave part of the stem intact with the fruit.*

*Eggplant are heavy and need support to prevent damage to the plant*

*Harvesting the eggplant promptly allows the plant to concentrate its energy on those that are still growing*

## Things to watch out for...

**Small fruit** Regular watering will encourage the fruit to develop fully—it is important that plants receive a constant supply of water while the eggplant are swelling. Once the first flowers appear, start applying a high potassium fertilizer rather than a general-purpose fertilizer, because this will encourage the fruit to form.

**Sagging stems** Eggplant are heavy fruit, and so the plants will need regular staking and support with strings to ensure that the stems don't snap and cause damage to the crop.

**Competing weeds** Keep the area around the plant well weeded to prevent competition for water and nutrients. If you are growing the plants in the vegetable patch, hoe regularly around them.

# Grow Asparagus

The young, tender spears of this delicious perennial plant are considered by many to be a gourmet treat. Patience is the key—the plant should not be harvested for at least three years, but the rewards will be worth the wait.

full sun

light soil

## Equipment

- Asparagus crowns
- Well-rotted manure
- Spade
- Fork
- Rake
- Bamboo poles and string
- Scissors
- Watering can
- General-purpose liquid fertilizer
- Asparagus knife

**Watering can**

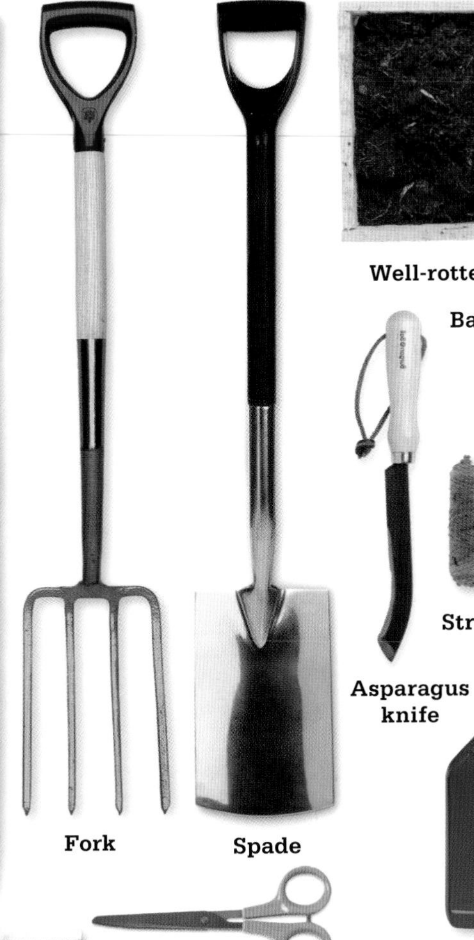

**Well-rotted manure**

**Bamboo poles**

**String**

**Asparagus knife**

**Fork**

**Spade**

**Rake**

**Scissors**

**Liquid fertilizer**

**Asparagus** *3 years until harvest*

**Prepare** *your site well before planting, in early spring*

**Plant** *the asparagus crowns into trenches in springtime*

**After three years,** *harvest for about 10 weeks in early spring*

**1** It is very important to think about where you place your asparagus plants, since they can remain in the ground for up to 20 years. Dig in plenty of well-rotted manure or compost in the season before planting and make sure the ground is well prepared (see p.15).

**Tip** Asparagus plants can be grown from seed, but it is far easier to buy them as bare-root crowns in the springtime.

*Dig the soil over with a spade, ensuring that all perennial weeds are removed*

*Break up the soil well*

**2** Once your soil has been thoroughly prepared, dig out a trench that is 12in (30cm) wide and 6in (15cm) deep. You can use a draw hoe or spade to do this.

**Tip** Sprinkle general purpose potting mix into the bottom of the trench to give the plants a boost when they start to grow.

**3** Create a mound on the floor of the trench. The peak of the ridge should be just below the level of the surrounding soil. Place the crowns on top of the ridge, 6in (15cm) apart, so that their tips are level with the soil's surface. Backfill the trench with soil.

**Why?** Growing the crowns on a mound helps drainage. If your soil is sandy then there is no need to plant in this way.

*Spread the crowns on the mound, with the middle of the plant at the highest point*

*The crowns should fit comfortably within the width of the trench*

Keep harvesting the spears for up to ten weeks
Hold the spear carefully as you cut to prevent it from snapping

**4** Asparagus spears should only be harvested after they have been in the ground for more than three years. Any earlier, and the plants won't be able to establish roots and will die. Use an asparagus knife to cut the spears just below the level of the soil.

**Tip** Use pruners if you don't have an asparagus knife.

## Caring for your **Asparagus**

This luxury crop is easy to grow once established. If the ground is prepared thoroughly prior to planting, it should reward you with delicious spears for many years.

### Things to watch out for...

**Ferny foliage** After ten weeks of harvesting, stop to allow the plant's ferny foliage to develop. The foliage will turn yellow in fall, at which point it should be cut down at ground level and added to the compost heap.

**Asparagus beetle** Keep an eye out for the bright-red asparagus beetle and remove by hand if you find it.

**Sagging plants** The tall foliage can be staked to prevent it from flopping over other plants in the garden (see p.77).

**Weeds** Make sure you keep the asparagus beds weed-free. They should also be mulched with organic matter each year in fall to help retain moisture. Add a general purpose fertilizer each spring.

Asparagus takes a few years to establish, but it's worth the wait

# Grow Globe Artichokes

Globe artichokes are a delicious gourmet treat, and their silvery, thistlelike plants will also be an attractive addition to the garden. Site them carefully, because these stately plants are a long term investment and should not be harvested until their second year.

full sun

moist soil

## Equipment

- Globe artichoke seeds or offsets
- Seed flats
- General-purpose potting mix
- Propagator
- Plastic pots
- Watering can
- Fork
- Rake
- Well-rotted manure
- Pruners

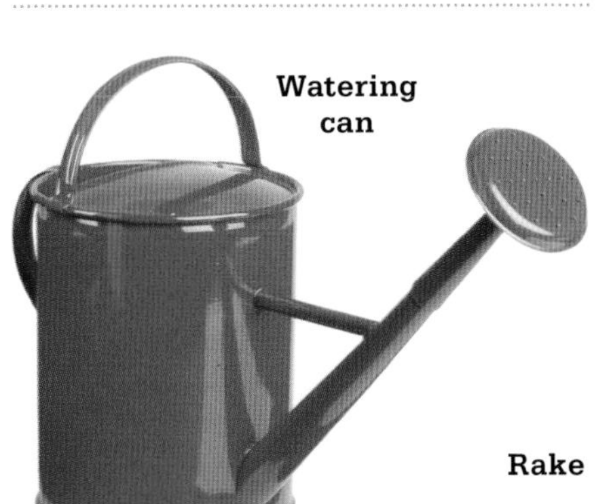
Watering can

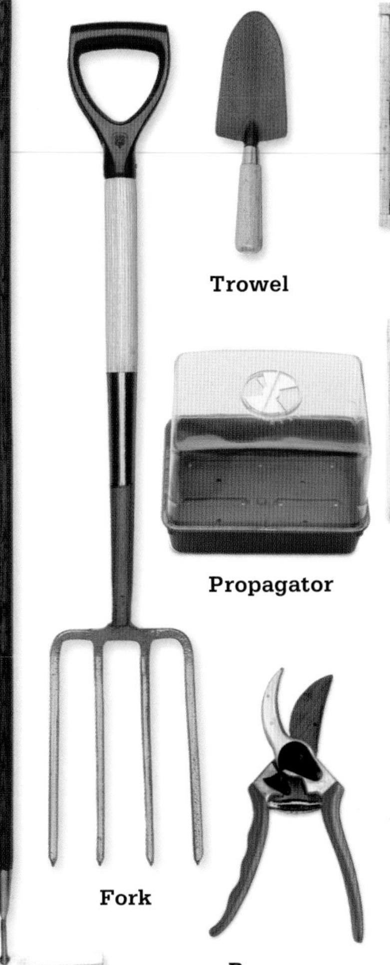
Trowel

Propagator

Fork

Rake

Pruners

General-purpose potting mix

Well-rotted manure

Seed flats

Plastic pots

**Globe artichokes** *1 year until harvest*

**Sow** *the seeds from late winter to spring and keep them warm*

**Repot them** *in late spring after hardening off*

**Harvest** *the heads from late spring to early summer*

**1** Sow the seeds ¾in (2cm) deep and the same distance apart. Water them in well, and keep warm. Once they have begun to develop, they can be repotted.

**Tip** Although it is possible to raise globe artichokes from seed, or to buy them as cuttings from a mature plant, or offsets, the simplest way to get started is to buy a young plant from a garden center.

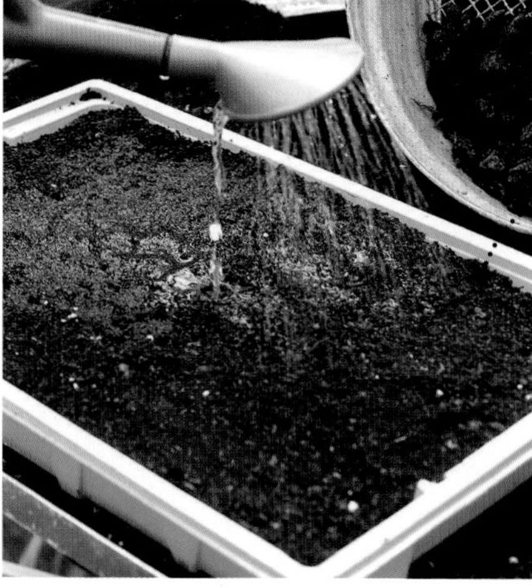

*The seeds should be placed in a heated propagator to encourage germination*

*Place the plants outside during the day for ten days to harden them off*

**2** The seedlings, whether you have bought them or grown them, will be ready to plant out in late spring. Harden them off (see p.74) and prepare the soil for them by removing all weeds and digging in plenty of well-rotted manure. Plant globe artichokes at a spacing of 5ft (1.5m). In the first few months, ensure that you keep the plants well watered to encourage them to establish strong roots.

**3** The globe artichokes are ready to harvest once they reach about the size of an apple, but while the scales are still tight—over time these will begin to open to make way for the flowers. Cut the artichoke from the stem, using a sharp knife or pruners.

**Tip** The plant may produce buds on the sideshoots, and a second crop once you begin to harvest.

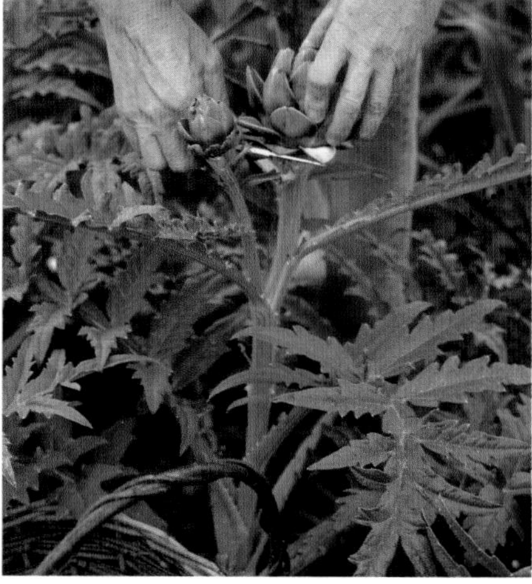

*Take care when cutting as the stems are tough and woody*

Use pruners to make a clean cut through the thick stems

**4** Because globe artichokes are perennial plants and can last for several years, it is important to take care of them over the winter, since a cold spell can kill them. Cut the stems back to ground level and then cover the plant with a thick mulch of straw or bark chips.

**Tip** In spring, once the risk of frost has passed, simply move the mulch aside and dig it into the soil.

## Caring for your **Globe artichokes**

This gourmet vegetable is well worth the effort, and once the plants are established, they will provide you with delicious crops for several years.

### Things to watch out for...

**Blackflies** This common pest can plague a globe artichoke plant, swarming the flower buds and stems, sucking the sap out, and disfiguring new growth. Wash the pests from the plant if you can, and consider using an appropriate insecticide. Keep plants well fed and watered to help them recover. Generally globe artichokes are disease free.

Globe artichokes are regal plants and would be an attractive addition to a flowerbed

# Create an Herb Parterre

A parterre is a formally designed herb, flower, or vegetable bed, grown in a small space. Edged by evergreen hedges, they are typically grown using a palette of different shades of foliage and are an attractive and delicious addition to the garden. Choose your favorite herbs and create your own pattern.

full sun

light soil

## Equipment

Assorted herb plants, such as rosemary, lavender, and thyme, a bay tree, and small boxwood plants

Horticultural grit

Spade

Rake

Weed-suppressing membrane

Gloves

Measuring tape

Chalk and short stakes or pegs

Utility knife

Trowel

Slate chips

Watering can

Pruners

**Weed-suppressing membrane**

**Gloves**

**Slate**

**Utility knife**

**Herb plants**

**Trowel**

**Spade**

**Rake**

**Pruners**

**Horticultural grit**

**Herbs** *4–16 weeks until harvest*

**Prepare your soil** *with grit in mid- to late spring*

**Plant out** *in late spring to early summer*

**Pinch back** *the boxwood plants in midsummer*

**Harvest** *leaves as you need them throughout the year*

**1** Herbs thrive in dry sites, which means that they need a free-draining soil. Dig over the soil and add about a bucket of grit per 10sq ft (1 square meter) and dig it into the soil.

**Remember** Heavy clay soils will need extra attention and more grit—water is very slow to drain through them (see pp.12–13).

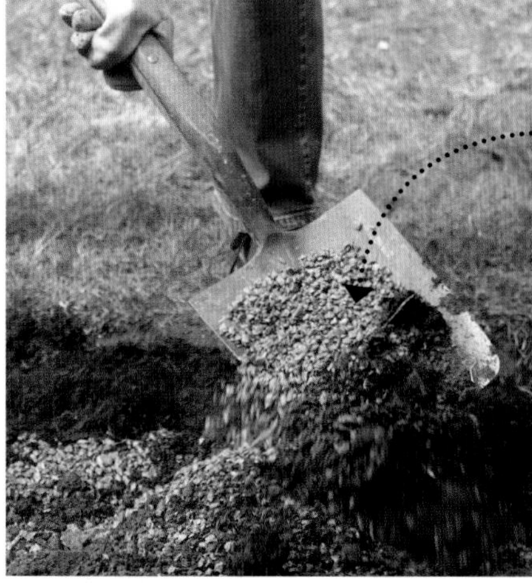

*Grit improves drainage by creating air spaces within the soil structure*

*Use a rake to level the ground before planting*

*Remove any large rocks or remaining weed roots from the surface*

**2** After incorporating the grit, rake the soil level and remove any stones or weeds. The best tool for doing this job is a large-headed, stainless steel landscape rake. Walk over the ground in both directions to remove any air pockets, and lightly rake again.

**Careful!** Remove any perennial weeds you come across—any root pieces will quickly germinate.

**3** Check that the area is now level—use a bubble level if you would like to be exact—then lay a weed barrier across the soil. This fabric should prevent weeds from germinating as well as preserve soil moisture, reducing your need to water.

**Tip** Use a spade to dig the edges of the fabric into the soil to hold it securely in place.

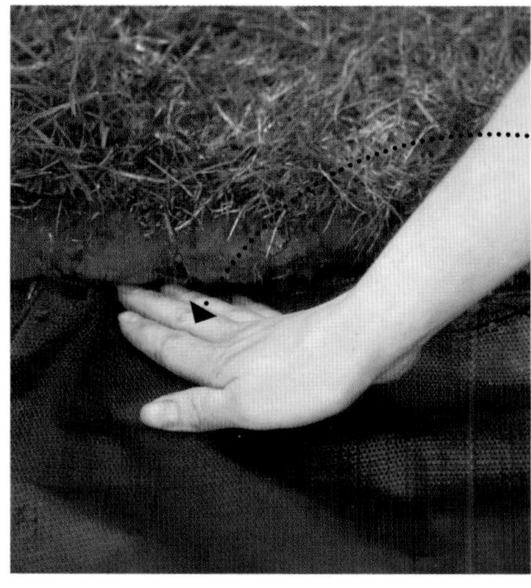

*Landscape fabric will help prevent weeds from germinating, which will spoil your design*

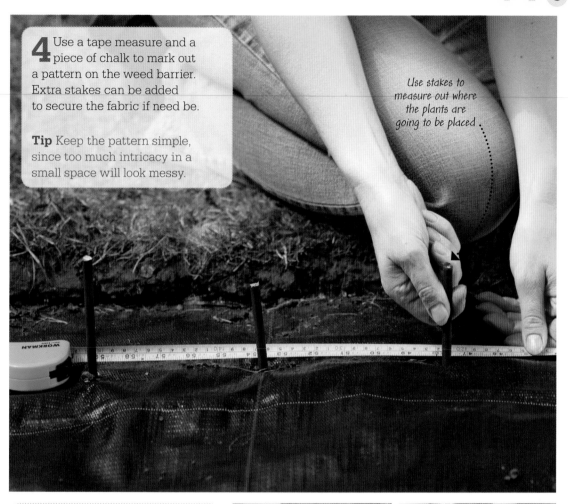

**4** Use a tape measure and a piece of chalk to mark out a pattern on the weed barrier. Extra stakes can be added to secure the fabric if need be.

**Tip** Keep the pattern simple, since too much intricacy in a small space will look messy.

*Use stakes to measure out where the plants are going to be placed*

**5** Following your chalk pattern, use a sharp knife to create small planting holes in the fabric for the boxwood edging plants—space them 8in (20cm) apart. Use a trowel to dig a hole in the soil underneath the membrane and plant them through it. Firm the plants in well with your fingers.

**6** Continue to plant out the boxwood hedging, following the pattern drawn on the fabric until all the plants are in the ground. Lay out the herb plants while they are in their pots. Play around with the positioning until you get an arrangement with which you are happy.

**Tip** Use larger plants, such as the bay, in attractive terra-cotta pots to create a central focal point.

**7** Once you are happy with the positioning of the herbs, plant them using the same technique given in step five. Use a brush to sweep the excess soil off the landscape fabric. Place slate chips over the surface to hide the holes and create an attractive finish to the parterre.

**Tip** Trim back any leggy herbs by a third to encourage bushy growth.

Gravel or stone chips can be used instead of slate

# Caring for your **Herb Parterre**

The herb parterre is ideal outside a kitchen window. Once created, it should be easy to maintain and will provide a constant supply of herbs for the kitchen.

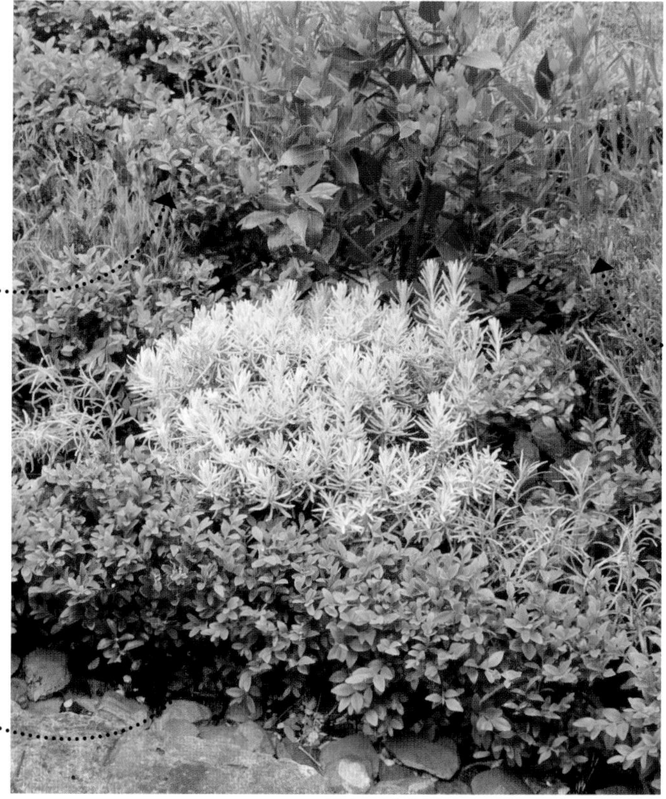

*Lavender provides attractive flowers as well as aromatic foliage*

*Rosemary adds to the evergreen structure of the planting design*

*Boxwood plants have been used to create this edging*

## Things to watch out for...

**Weeds** The landscape fabric laid over the planting beds should ensure that the parterre remains largely weed-free, but it will still need checking and weeding occasionally. Avoid using a hoe because this will rip the fabric.

**Overwatering** These herb plants come from the Mediterranean and will therefore require minimal watering once established. However, they will need watering for a few weeks after planting.

**Missing mulch** Look out for gaps in the slate mulch on the surface of the parterre; it will need topping off every couple of years.

**Straggly plants** Lavender and rosemary can be cut back lightly after flowering. Do not prune back into the older wood on lavender since it won't grow back. Boxwood hedging should be clipped back neatly after the risk of cold is over to keep these structural plants looking straight and formal.

**Lawn edges** If the parterre has been created in a lawn, the edges of the grass around the parterre will need regular cutting back to prevent it from encroaching on the plants.

# Plant Blueberries in a Pot

Blueberries are ideal for containers—they need an acidic soil, and you can provide this far more easily if you grow them in a pot rather than in an open bed. Blueberries will produce an abundant crop of succulent, juicy berries and will also provide white spring flowers and a dazzling display of red and orange foliage in the fall.

## Equipment

- Blueberry plant
- Acidic potting mix
- Large container
- Crocks
- Watering can
  plants must be watered with rainwater to maintain acidity
- Chelated iron fertilizer

**Blueberries** *8–10 weeks until harvest*

**Pot up** *your blueberry plants in either fall or spring*

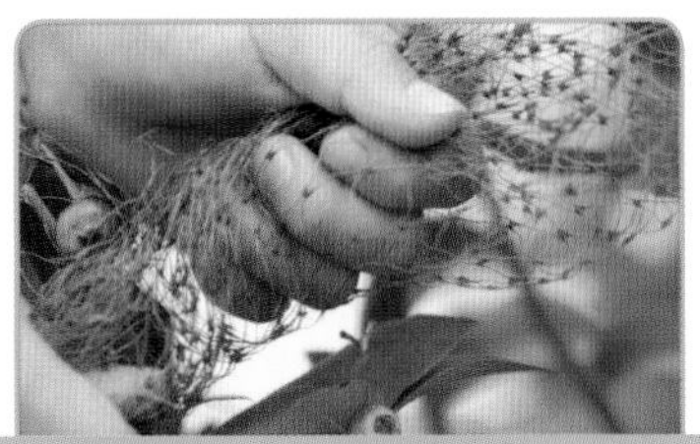

**Protect** *the fruit from hungry birds, using netting*

**Harvest** *the berries from late summer and into early fall*

**1** Remove the blueberry plant from its plastic pot and soak it in a bucket of rainwater for about 20 minutes prior to planting. Select an attractive container about 15in (38cm) wide and cover the bottom with crocks for drainage. Put a layer of high-quality, acidic potting mix in the bottom of the container and place the plastic pot on top of it. Fill around the pot with soil mix.

*Acidic soil suits acid-loving plants*

*Make sure the container is cold-resistant*

*Do not overfill the container, or soil will run off when watering*

**2** Push the potting mix around the pot and firm it down by hand. Make sure the mix is just below the rim of the container so that it will be level with the top of the blueberry's root ball.

**Remember** Before you plant the blueberry, move the pot to its final location in a sunny, sheltered spot. Once it is filled, it will be too heavy to move easily.

**3** Remove the plastic pot from the container and place the plant in the hole created—the root ball will fit in perfectly. Ensure the top of the root ball sits level with the surface of the soil mix.

**Careful!** Do not mulch the top of the pot with manure since this can alter the acidity of the potting mix. Instead add a mulch of pebbles, gravel, slate, shells, or pea gravel.

*Gently tease out the roots before planting*

**4** Your plant will need netting in summer to prevent birds from stealing the berries—construct a tepee from decorative sticks (see pp.106–110) and hang the netting from this.

**Careful!** Plants need watering with rainwater since it is more acidic than tap water. To collect it, rig up a rain barrel to collect the runoff from a shed or house.

*Ensure that the netting is secured at the bottom to keep out intruders*

## Caring for your **Blueberries**

Blueberries thrive in moist, acidic soil in full sun—ensure that you give them acidic potting mix and water them with rainwater to keep them happy and healthy.

### Things to watch out for...

**Garden thieves** Birds can rapidly strip a plant of its berries and are the most likely threat to your crop, so make sure you rig up some netting to protect the plant when the fruit starts to ripen.

**Spindly growth** Lightly prune blueberry plants in early spring before they come into new growth. Remove some of the older wood at the base of the plant and cut back any dead or damaged growth (see pp.176–179 for further information).

*Pick the berries when the fruit has turned blue*

**Also learn to grow** ▸▸▸

# How to grow **Strawberries in a Container**

full sun

light soil

## Equipment

- 10 strawberry plants
- Terra-cotta strawberry planter
- General-purpose potting mix
- Crocks
- Slow-release compost
- Watering can

The trailing habit of strawberries makes them perfect for growing in planters. With good care, they should produce fruit for two or three years.

### PLANTING

**Buy strawberry plants** in early spring. Place crocks over the drainage holes at the bottom of the planter and cover them up with a layer of potting mix that reaches just below the bottom level of the planting holes. Place the strawberry plants through the planting holes so that their root balls set inside the container. Once they are in position, add more mix until the second set of holes is reached and repeat the process. Finally, plant one or two strawberry plants in the top and firm in, ensuring that the soil mix level is just below the top of the container. Water in well. Be careful not to overfill the planter, otherwise water will run right off the surface when you water the plants.

### LOCATION

**Place the planter** in a sheltered location on a patio in full sun. Stand the container on bricks, because this will help with drainage.

### CARE

**As soon as flowers** start to appear on the plants they will need a weekly high-potassium liquid fertilizer, such as tomato fertilizer.

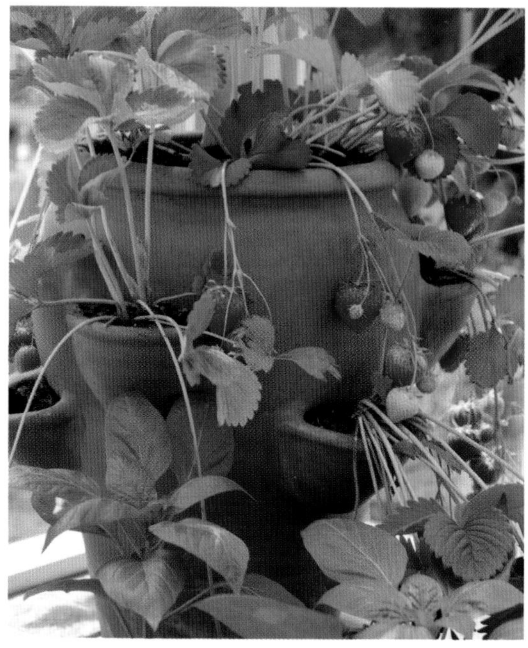

### HARVESTING

**The harvest period** depends on the type of strawberries. Summer-fruiting strawberries bear fruit from late spring to midsummer, depending on whether they are early, mid, or late varieties. Everbearing strawberries produce lighter yields but fruit throughout summer and into early fall. Pick when the fruit turns red, retaining the stem.

### AFTER HARVESTING

**Water the plants** every day during the summer. Ensure you soak them thoroughly, or the plants on the bottom level will remain dry. Old, ragged foliage should be cut back with pruners to expose the newer young foliage.

### OVERWINTERING

**Strawberries will benefit** from being moved to a cool greenhouse during winter, or can be left on a porch or in a sheltered location. The plants should produce fruit for two or three more years, although yields will dwindle over time.

# How to plant **a Pear Tree in a Pot**

full sun

light soil

## Equipment

- A pear tree
- Large, deep container
- Soil-based potting mix
- Crocks
- Controlled-release fertilizer
- Pruners

Pear trees are a beautiful addition to a garden, with their spring blossoms and delicious, succulent fruit. Keeping the tree in a pot ensures that it stays small and compact, making picking the fruit easy.

### PLANTING

**Take the tree out of its pot** and soak it in a bucket of water for an hour before planting. Add a layer of crocks to the bottom of the container and place a layer of soil mix on top. Tease out some of the roots before placing the tree in the container, ensuring that the top of the root ball sets about 2in (5cm) below the top of the pot.

**Position the pear tree** in the center of the container and make sure it is upright and straight. Pack the soil mix around the root ball, making sure it comes up to the same level on the trunk as it did in the original pot. Water the tree in well.

### CARE

**Keep the tree well watered,** especially during summer, when the pot will dry out quickly. Birds love to peck the ripening fruit, so cover the tree up with a net as the fruitlets start to develop. The tree should be repotted into fresh soil mix every two or three years. Scrape at the root ball with a knife to stimulate new growth and add fresh fertilizer at the recommended rate. Mulch each year with manure.

### HARVESTING

**The tree should crop** each summer. Be careful not to bruise the fruit when picking. Generally, pears are best picked when slightly underripe and allowed to ripen indoors, but check which variety you have to see whether fruit should be eaten immediately or are better stored for a few weeks.

### PRUNING

**Pear trees will benefit** from a light prune each winter to encourage new growth. Remove crossing branches and anything that looks dead or diseased. Thin out the fruitlets in summer to encourage the tree to produce larger fruit.

# Plant a Plum Tree

Delicious, juicy plums that can be eaten straight from the tree are a treat in summertime. Choose a self-pollinating variety on a semidwarfing rootstock if you are short of space. You will need to protect your plum tree from cold and prune it in spring or summer to keep it in shape.

full sun

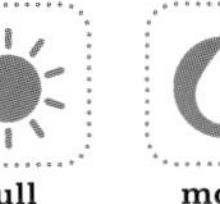
moist soil

## Equipment

- Plum tree
- Fork
- Well-rotted manure
- Rake
- Tree stake and tree tie
- Watering can
- General-purpose liquid fertilizer
- Pruners

**Plums** *14–16 weeks until harvest*

**Plant** *bare-root trees in fall or spring; potted trees any time*

**Mulch** *the tree with organic matter after planting in spring*

**Thin out** *the young fruitlets in early summer*

**Harvest** *the plump, ripe fruit in mid- to late summer*

**1** Plum trees are best planted in the fall when the soil is still warm. This gives them a chance to settle before they start growing in spring. Dig a hole large enough to hold the root ball. Make sure the root ball is at the same level in the ground as it was in the pot. If it is planted too deeply, the trunk will rot; if too shallowly, the root ball will dry out.

Make sure the tree is straight when planting it

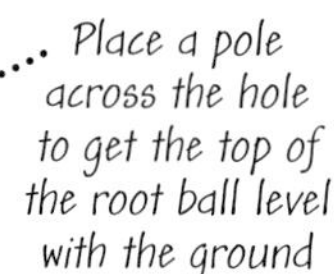

Place a pole across the hole to get the top of the root ball level with the ground

**2** Insert your tree stake before you plant your tree. Place the tree in the hole and fill around it using the soil you dug out—mix in some fertilizer as you do so, to ensure that the plant will be well-fed as it grows. Tie the tree firmly to the stake, using a tree tie.

**Careful!** It is vital to insert your stake in the ground before you plant your tree, otherwise you risk damaging the roots.

**3** Once the tree is planted, add a layer of well-rotted manure or compost to the area above the root system. The layer should be about 2in (5cm) thick but should not be allowed to touch the trunk, since it could cause it to rot.

**Why?** This mulch will help retain moisture in the soil during the summer and suppress weeds.

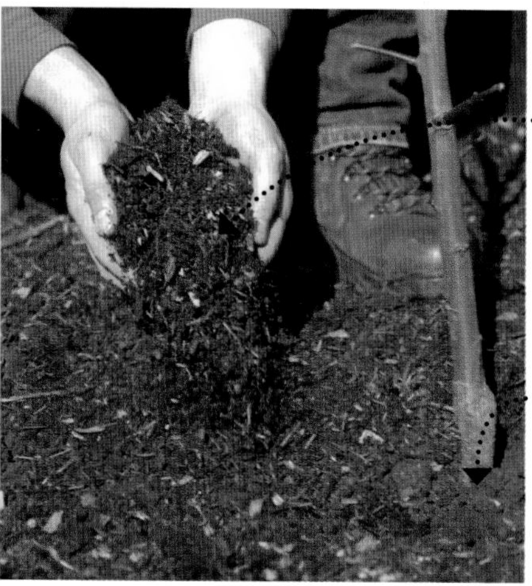

Make sure the mulch is evenly scattered

Keep the mulch 2in (5cm) away from the trunk to prevent the tree from rotting

4 New plum trees require regular watering until they are well rooted. Established trees are more drought-tolerant, but yield better if watered during dry spells. Mulch the tree again in spring with organic matter and apply a granular fertilizer.

*Water the root area of the tree thoroughly after planting*

*In the first year, remove fruitlets early in the season*

*When the tree is mature, aim to leave about 3in (8cm) between fruit when thinning*

5 The plum tree should not be allowed to fruit for the first couple of years after planting—you want it to first produce its roots and develop branches. This means that you will need to remove all the fruitlets when they appear.

**Remember** In subsequent years, fruit should be thinned in early summer—this will result in fewer but larger, better-quality fruit.

6 Fruit should be ready for picking between mid- to late summer, depending on the variety. Plums on the same tree may ripen at different times, so do a number of pickings on the same tree.

**Careful!** Never prune trees in wintertime. Wait for the buds to open before pruning in spring or late summer. Use pruners to clip small branches and a pruning saw for the large ones.

*Plums are ready for picking when the flesh is slightly soft*

# Caring for your **Plum Tree**

Fresh plums are delicious in summer. With careful attention, a plum tree will make a beautiful and long-lasting addition to your garden.

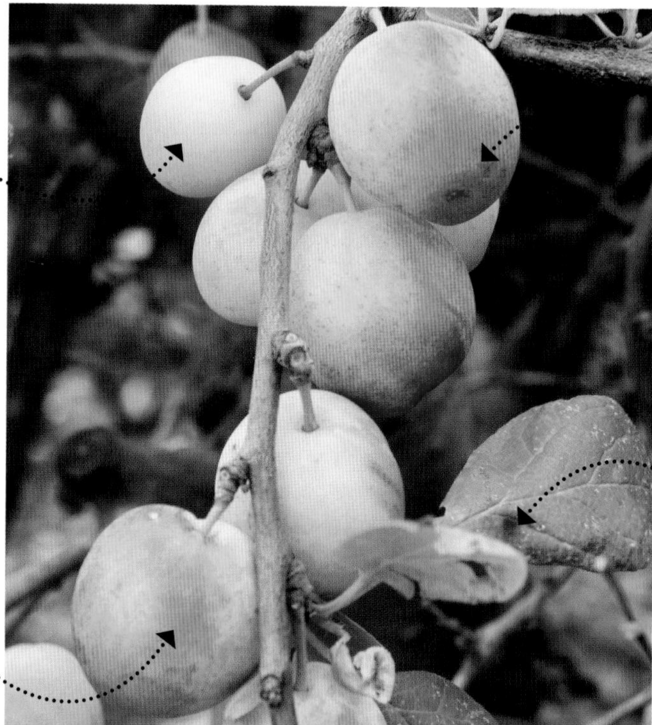
This unripe fruit needs to remain on the tree until it is ripe.
This plum is ready for picking when soft and in full color
Regularly check the leaves for signs of pests
Remove some fruit if you are concerned the branches are going to snap under the weight.

## Things to watch out for...

**Dry soil** Newly planted plums should be watered regularly during the summer. In subsequent years, they will only need watering during dry periods. Plum trees planted in the yard will benefit from a granular general-purpose fertilizer spread around their root systems in spring, followed by an annual mulch of well-rotted manure around the base.

**Frost** The blossoms can be damaged by cold as they start to form in springtime. If possible, protect the tree by draping fabric over it at night.

**Garden thieves** The sweet, ripening fruit is irresistible to birds, so throw a net over the tree in midsummer to prevent them from attacking the fruit. Wasps may also become a problem, so hang a jelly jar filled with some jelly and water nearby, to draw them away from your crop.

**Crowded branches** Plum trees should only be pruned when they are growing, in spring or summer. Never prune when the tree is dormant during winter, since the open wounds make it susceptible to disease. Remove any congested or damaged growth (see pp.176–179).

**Also learn to grow** ▸▸▸

# How to plant a **Cherry Tree**

full sun

light soil

## Equipment

- A cherry tree
- Spade
- Well-rotted manure
- Tree stake and tie
- Netting
- General-purpose fertilizer
- Pruners

### TREE SELECTION

**If you are restricted** for space, choose a self-pollinating cherry tree such as 'Stella', since it will not need another tree for pollination; some varieties will not produce a crop without another tree nearby to fertilize them, so plan carefully. Make sure that the tree is on a dwarf rootstock such as colt or gisela 5 or 6. This will ensure it doesn't grow too big, which will make pruning and harvesting easier. Choose a sweet cherry, which you can eat raw, or a sour cherry, which is good for cooking.

### PLANTING

**Select a sheltered**, sunny spot. Dig out a hole double the width of the root ball and the same depth. Push in a vertical stake at the side of the hole. Place the tree in the hole and backfill with a mix of well-rotted manure and excavated soil; general-purpose fertilizer can also be mixed in. Mulch around the base of the tree and tie it to the stake using a tree tie. Water the tree well.

### CARE

**Don't allow the tree** to fruit in the first two years—remove the young fruitlets by hand. This will give the tree time to develop a strong root system and branch structure. Harvest fruit in the third year. Use a net to protect the fruit from birds.

### PRUNING

**Sweet and sour cherries** both need pruning in spring or summer, but have different pruning needs; it is important to know which type of tree you are dealing with or you may end up removing the fruit-bearing spurs by accident. Sweet cherries form fruit-bearing spurs on older wood, so leave some of this when pruning and cut back the newer growth by half to prevent congestion and a shady canopy. Sour cherries bear their fruit on wood produced the previous year. To prune a sour cherry, cut away some of the older wood and leave newer wood to produce fruit later that year.

# Basic Pruning

Pruning should be carried out on woody plants such as trees and shrubs at least once a year, and sometimes two or three times, for a variety of reasons. It tidies up the plant, encourages fresh growth, relieves congestion, and allows sunlight to reach into the canopy. Most importantly, it allows you to remove dead, diseased, or dying branches.

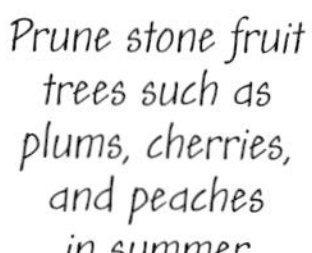

Prune stone fruit trees such as plums, cherries, and peaches in summer

It is worth spending money on a good set of pruners

**Pruning wayward stems**

**Pruning to improve appearance**

**Pruning out crossing branches**

## Pruning congested plants

Fruit trees depend on sunlight to ripen their buds and produce a regular crop. Prune out crossing branches, since not only will they rub on each other, causing wounds and entry points for disease, but they also create too much shade. This will cause leggy growth at the expense of fruit. Ensuring that plants are not congested will also allow air to circulate around the canopy, which will help to prevent a buildup of diseases such as mildew.

This swollen bud will no longer produce fruit due to the branch damage
This old pruning wound is perfect—it is clean and was cut back to another healthy branch
This split branch needs to be removed and cut back to a lower section

**Split branches susceptible to disease**

This area is congested so the spurs and branches should be thinned out
Always make a clean cut when pruning to avoid a jagged edge that could become diseased

**Using a pruning saw to remove diseased branches**

## Pruning diseased plants

Diseased branches may look corky, withered, pitted, or even have growths on them; foliage may be yellow, brown, mottled, or dead. If the affected branches are not removed promptly, they will pass on their infection to the rest of the plant and eventually kill it. Always make a clean pruning cut back to a healthy section of wood. When cutting away diseased material, make sure the saw or pruners are sterilized afterward to keep the problem from spreading.

Blueberries

Fall-fruiting raspberries

## Pruning for productivity

If left unpruned, plants may produce small, tasteless fruit and will eventually become a tangled mess of shoots and branches. It is important to keep fruit trees and bushes well-pruned so that sunlight can reach the fruiting buds—it promotes the formation and ripening of fruit. Careful pruning also encourages plants to produce a large yield, which will be easier to harvest from a well-tended plant. Different types of fruit require pruning in specific ways to maximize the amount of fruit they produce. For example, blueberries fruit on younger wood, so should be lightly pruned in winter or very early spring. You will need to remove some of the older branches and leave the majority of the younger wood on the plants. Alternatively, summer-fruiting raspberries should have their old canes removed at ground level after fruiting, leaving just the new canes in place, while fall-fruiting raspberries should have all their stems cut to ground level in early spring. In spring, new shoots will emerge. Always check your plant's needs before you prune.

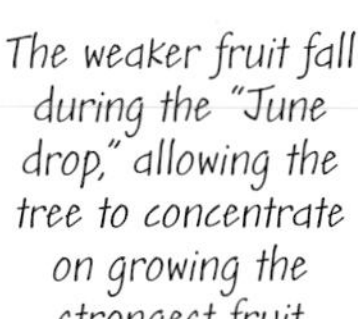

The weaker fruit fall during the "June drop," allowing the tree to concentrate on growing the strongest fruit

Fallen fruit should be removed immediately before it attracts wasps and harbors diseases


## The "June drop"

In midsummer, trees naturally shed some of their fruit. This ensures they don't overcrop and exhaust themselves. It also prevents their branches from becoming overladen with heavy fruit and snapping. Once the drop is finished, fruit can be thinned again, if necessary.

After pruning, use oil on a rag to remove the sap and sawdust from the teeth of the blade


## Caring for your tools

Clean your tools with household disinfectant before and after each use to avoid spreading diseases from one plant to the other. Wipe saws with some oil on a rag and sharpen pruners by rubbing a sharpener across the blade, to ensure a clean cut when pruning.

# Pruning Shapes

If you want to become a first-class gardener, why not train your fruit trees into different shapes? A trained tree takes up less space and can bear more fruit than a free-standing type. All you need are the proper timings and techniques. Here are some of the most eye-catching styles.

**Tip** Cordons that are tilted at 45 degrees are called oblique cordons, and produce an equal amount of fruit along the trunk. The advantage of cordons is that you can grow lots of different varieties in a small space.

## Cordons

These grow on a single stem with short, stubby fruiting spurs along their length. Cordons should be pruned in late summer. Prune back the new growth to one or two buds, but allow the leading shoot to grow until it has reached the desired height. This technique means that varieties that bear fruit on the tips would lose their fruit for the next year, so select tree varieties that produce fruit on spurs and not on the tips of new growth.

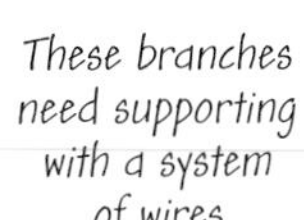

These branches need supporting with a system of wires

## Espaliers

An espalier has a central trunk with a series of parallel horizontal tiers growing out from it. It adds wonderful ornamental value to the garden. You can create as many tiers as the vigor of the tree will allow, although most commonly there are four or five tiers. Prune in late summer, cutting back the new growth to a spot two buds from the branches.

Unlike cordons and espaliers, standard apple trees should be pruned in winter
Choose a dwarfing rootstock to keep the tree small and compact


## Semidwarfs

This is the most commonly seen tree shape. Semidwarfs have a small, branch-free leg about 20in (50cm) high. Above this, the canopy branches out into the shape of an open-centered goblet. Prune when the tree is dormant, in winter. To keep the open shape, remove any crossing stems in the center of the tree to allow sunlight into the canopy.

# Store Carrots in Soil

Carrots are easy to grow, but keeping them crunchy and fresh over winter can be a little trickier—once they have been dug up, it is important to store them as quickly as possible since the air can cause them to become soft.

**1** If stored correctly, carrots can be kept in a cardboard box for a few months. All you will need is a sturdy cardboard box, some old newspaper, and some soil-based potting mix. Remove all the green leaves and foliage on the carrots, since these will draw moisture away from the root. Place a layer of newspaper and a 1-in (2.5-cm) thick layer of potting mix into the box.

*Place newspaper or paper towels in the bottom of the box first*

*Avoid using soil from your garden that could have pests and slugs in it*

*Space carrots out evenly in the box, ensuring they don't touch each other*

**2** Double-check the carrots for any defects or diseased parts. One bad carrot can quickly rot and contaminate the rest of the crop. Lay the carrots on the soil, spacing them out so that they are not in contact with each other.

**3** Cover the first layer of carrots with another layer of soil mix, also 1in (2.5cm) thick. Place another layer of carrots on top and repeat this process until the box is full.

**Careful!** The cardboard box should be stored in a cool, well-ventilated, rodent-free place such as a shed or garage.

*Keep creating layers of carrots until you reach the top of the box*

*Once placed in storage, it should be checked regularly for rotting crops*

# How to **Store Crops**

## WRAPPING IN PAPER

**Apples** will keep for a few months if wrapped in paper and kept in a cool, dark place. Some varieties of apples store better than others, so check before you harvest. Use tissue paper to prevent the fruit becoming damaged in storage —any cuts or bruises will quickly cause the fruit to rot. Alternatively, lay the apples out on trays so that their skins aren't touching. Check the fruit regularly to ensure that it hasn't started to rot.

**Storing apples in paper**

## DRYING

**You can dry fruit and vegetables** in different ways: a variety of crops such as apples, plums, parsnips, and tomatoes can be dried in the oven on a very low heat, while crops such as beans, chiles, and herbs can be air-dried.

**To oven-dry apples,** wash, core, and slice them into rings and rinse them in 1 pint (473ml) of water with 2 tbsp lemon juice mixed in. Dry the rings off with a dish towel and then arrange them on wire cooling racks placed on baking trays. Place them in the oven for 8–24 hours on the lowest heat, turning them occasionally. When you are happy with the texture, remove them from the oven, leave them to stand for a few hours, and then seal them in an airtight container.

**To air-dry chiles,** harvest the peppers with a small amount of stem attached. Knot them onto a string and hang them up in a warm, dry place for a few weeks, until they are shriveled.

**Drying apples**

## MAKING JAMS AND PRESERVES

**Cooking and canning** your extra crops is another excellent way of storing them, especially if you have a glut of crops that you don't want to waste. Almost any fruit or vegetable can be converted into a delicious jam or chutney, so find a recipe that looks appealing, and get cooking!

## STORING IN BAGS

**Root crops** such as potatoes will store well if they are dried, placed in double layered paper bags, and kept in a cool, frost-free place. Make sure that the tubers are completely dry before you store them, to prevent them from rotting. Ensure that light is not allowed to reach them.

**Alternatively,** root crops such as rutabagas can be stored in a homemade "clamp." In a sheltered corner of your garden, lay a thick layer of straw on the ground and pile your crops on top of it to create a pyramid. Cover this with straw and then pack soil on top of it to keep the roots warm. Check the crops every now and then for signs of damage.

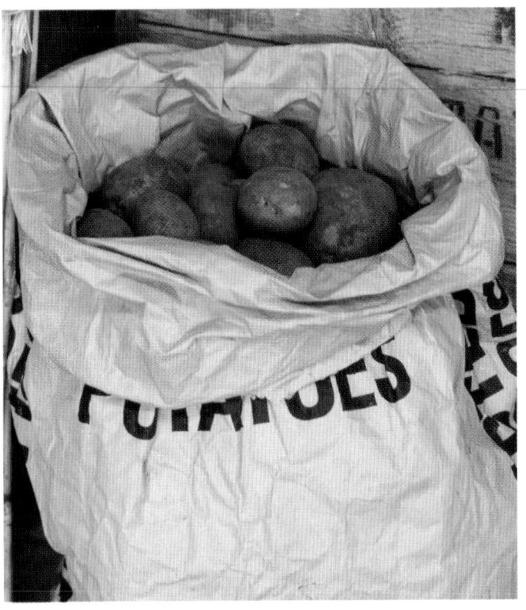

**Storing potatoes in a bag**

## FREEZING

**Some fruits and vegetables can be frozen** if you have a glut and enough room in your freezer to keep them. Some fruit can be frozen whole, such as raspberries, black currants, red currants, and blueberries. Strawberries will only be usable for purées, jams, or sauces after freezing. Fruit such as apples and pears need to be made into a purée before you freeze them.

**To freeze blueberries**, wash the fruit thoroughly and remove any that look diseased. Spread the fruit out on a baking tray, so that none of the berries are touching, and place it in the freezer. Once the fruit has frozen solid, transfer it into clean containers such as plastic boxes or zipper bags and store it in these. Freezing the fruit this way means that the berries will not freeze into a solid lump, and can be used individually once defrosted—you may feel this is unnecessary if you only intend to use the fruit for cooking.

**Vegetables such as beans and broccoli** will need to be blanched quickly before freezing. Boil them in water for a few minutes until soft and then immerse them in ice water to cool them quickly. Dry them off and then place in the freezer.

**Freezing blueberries**

# Index


## A

acidic potting mix 12, 14, 166, 167
acidic soil 14, 115, 164, 167
ammonia sulfate 125
annual crops 85, 93, 134
aphids 66, 92
apples 18
 drying and storing 184
 growing in pot 116–120
artichokes 154–157
asparagus 150–153
asparagus beetle 153

## B

baby vegetables
 beets 47
 leeks 138, 141
badgers 93
bag, zucchini in 82–85
bamboo poles, *see* poles
banana skins 65
bark mulch 76, 157
basil 35, 46
bay 162
beans 132, 133, 135
 drying 184
 freezing 185
 *see also* runner beans
beer traps 67
bees 109
beets 132, 133, 134
 baby beets in pots 47
 growing 98
bin, growing potatoes in 80–81
biodegradable pots 10, 140
birds 103, 104, 129
 protecting cabbage 103
 *see also* netting
black currants 122–125, 185
blackberries 19
blackflies 109, 157
blanching leeks 142
blight
 potato 81
 tomato 45, 65
blueberries 12, 14, 185
 growing in pot 164–167
bolting, spinach 41
bottle cloches 75, 87
boxwood hedging 161, 162, 163
broccoli 13, 14, 18, 100
 freezing 185
 purple sprouting 105, 133, 135
Brussels sprouts 13, 14, 18, 100, 135

## C

cabbage 13, 135
 growing 100–104
 pests 103, 128
cabbage collars 104, 105, 128
cabbage root flies 103, 104, 105, 128
cabbage white caterpillars 103, 104, 128
calendula flowers 40
canning 184
carrot rust flies 96, 97, 99, 129
carrots 13, 133, 134
 growing in container 16, 94–97
 pests 96, 97, 129
 resistant varieties 97
 storing in soil 182–183
caterpillars
 cabbage white 103
 gooseberry sawfly 127
 leek moth 143
 removing by hand 39, 103, 127
cauliflower 14, 18, 135
celery 135
cell packs 10, 102
cherries 175, 176
chiles 135, 184
chitting potatoes 80
chives in a pot 46
chlorophyll 22, 24
chloroplasts 23
clamp 185
clay soils 13, 160
cloches 19, 92, 110, 129
 types 75
clubroot 104, 135
cold frame 74, 75, 147
cold protection 124
 potatoes 81
 runner beans 106, 109, 110
collars 67, 104, 105, 128
compost bin 136
containers 10, 12, 14, 16–17
 carrots 94–97
 cold-proof 16, 118, 121
 drainage 32
 edible flowers 40
 peppers 91
 potatoes 80–81
 runner beans 106–110
 salad greens 38–39, 40
 spinach 41
 strawberries 168
 Swiss chard 41
 tomatoes 44–45
 watering 16, 32, 66
 *see also* pots; window boxes
copper tape 67
cordons 180
 currants 126
 gooseberries 127
 oblique cordons 180
 pruning 127
 vertical cordons 126
cranberries 12, 14
crocks 10, 46, 118
crop rotation 59, 134–135
currants
 black currants 122–125
 white and red currants 126
cut-and-come-again crops 40, 98

## D

damping down greenhouse 92
dandelions 69
deer 93
dibber 8, 30
digging 13, 15, 31
diseases 13, 66, 176, 179
 crop rotation 134, 135
 pruning diseased plants 177
dividing herbs 46, 50, 51
drainage
 containers 17, 32, 46
 hanging baskets 50, 51
 incorporating grit 50
drying produce 184

## E

easy-to-grow plot 132
edible flowers 40
eggplant 18, 34, 135
 growing 144–149
equipment 8–11
espaliers 181

## F

fabric 11
 cold protection 19, 124, 174
 pest control 55, 97, 99, 103, 129
family plot 133
fertilization 21
fertilizer 13, 24–25
 applying 68
 general 68
 granular 173, 174
 handling 84, 118
 high potassium 149
 liquid 39, 64, 85, 91, 103
 slow-release 62, 68, 118
 tomato 44, 45, 63, 65, 90, 168
fertilizing 24–25, 68
 black currants 125
 cabbage 103
 containers 16, 39, 120
 eggplant 148, 149
 peppers 90, 91
 strawberries 63, 64, 168
 zucchini 85
fig tree in pot 121
figure-eight knot 34
firming in 31, 124
flats, *see* seed flats
flowers
 blossoms 118, 169, 174
 edible 40, 85
 zucchini 85
fork 8, 15, 69, 81
freezing 185
frost 18, 19, 74, 75
 cloches 75, 129
 cold-proof containers 16, 118, 121
 fabric 124, 174
 fruit blossoms 174
 mulching 157
 planting out 30
fruit trees 19
 June drop 179
 pruning 176–178

see also individual types
furrows 38, 51, 72, 96

G
garden compost 31, 136
garden fabric, *see* fabric
garden hoses 33
garlic 56–59
gaseous exchange 22, 24
germination 20, 28, 38, 72
globe artichokes 154–157
gloves 9, 84, 99, 118
gooseberries 18, 127
gooseberry sawflies 127
green beans 132, 133
greenhouse
damping down 92
eggplant 147
overwintering strawberries 168
peppers 92
ventilation 92
watering 66
grit
adding to soil or potting mix 13, 50, 160
deterring slugs 67
groundsel 69
growing bags 91
growing conditions 20

H
hanging baskets 10, 12
growing herbs 48–51
growing strawberries 60–64
growing tomatoes 65
lining 50, 62
planting 50, 62
supports 62
turning 64
watering 51
hardening off 74
artichokes 156
eggplant 147
peppers 91
sweet corn 93
zucchini 84
hedges 19, 158, 161
heeling in 99, 143
herbs
drying 184
growing in baskets 48–51
growing in pots 46
herb parterre 158–163
perennial 51
hilling up
leeks 142, 143
potatoes 80, 81
sweet corn 93
hoe 8, 54
honeydew 92

I
indoor peppers 92
insecticide 45, 92, 157
interplanting 47
sweet corn and squash 93, 133

J
jams 184
jelly trap 64, 174
June drop 179

K
kale 100, 135
kitchen garden, planting plans 132–133
kitchen waste, recycling 136
knot, figure-eight 34

L
landscape fabric 11, 160–162, 163
lavender 163
leaf mold 76
making 137
leaves
avoiding compost on 76
avoiding water on 31, 32
making leaf mold 137
scorched 31, 85, 103
wilted 39, 51
yellow 115
*see also* salad greens
leek moth 143
leek rust 59, 143
leeks 133, 134, 138–143
baby 141
blanching 142
lettuce 16, 132, 133, 134
growing in window box 40
sowing in flats 28
life cycle 20–21
light energy 22–23
lime 14
liquid fertilizer
cabbage 103
hanging baskets 51, 64
peppers 91
window boxes 39
zucchini 85

M
manure
avoiding use of 54, 58, 166
digging in 13, 15, 31, 68, 102, 152
handling 84
mixing with potting mix 84
mulch 76, 119, 124, 174
marigolds 45
mice 110, 128
mildew 127, 176
herbs 51
zucchini 85
mint 50
mulching 76
acidic potting mix 166
asparagus beds 153
bark chips 76, 157
cold protection 157
compost 121
containers 11
fruit trees 172
manure 119, 124, 174
slate 162, 163
straw 76, 157

N
nasturtium flowers 40
netting 11, 39, 128
blueberries 167
broccoli 105
cabbage 104
currants 125, 126
figs 121
fruit trees 120, 169, 174
garlic 59
onion sets 54
peas 111
strawberries 64
sweet corn 93
nitrogen 25, 68, 125, 136
crop rotation 134, 135
north-facing garden 126
nutrients 13, 14, 24–25, 134, 137

O
onion fly 55, 143
onion hoe 54
onions 97, 132, 134
crop rotation 134
growing from sets 52–55
rot 54, 55
ornamental plants
cabbage 104
espaliers 181
globe artichokes 154, 157
runner beans 106
strawberry flowers 63
overwatering 58, 59, 163
overwintering
artichokes 157
strawberries 168

P
parsnips 13, 133, 134
drying 184
growing 99
heeling in 99
parterre, herb 158–163
peaches 176
pears 185
growing in pot 169
peas 111, 135
pebble mulch 76, 119
peppers 18
colors 91, 92
growing in pot 88–92
growing indoors 92
staking 77, 91
tying in 34
perennial plants
artichokes 157
asparagus 152
herbs 51
pests 66
crop rotation 134
protection 75, 128–129
pH testing 14
phosphorus 25, 68
photosynthesis 22–23
pinching back 35
eggplant 148
figs 121

peppers 90
sideshoots 35, 45
strawberry flowers 63
tips 35, 92, 109, 121
tomatoes 45
plaits 55, 59
planning a kitchen garden 132–33
plant growth 20–21
plant needs 24–25
planting
apple tree in pot 118–119
asparagus 152
in blocks 93
blueberries in pot 164–167
cherry tree 175
currants 122–125, 126
fig tree in pot 121
garlic 56–59
gooseberries 127
hanging baskets 50, 62
onion sets 52–55
pear tree in pot 169
plum tree 170–174
potatoes 78–81
sweet corn 93
planting bag, zucchini in 82–85
planting out 30–31
cabbage 102
depth 31
eggplant 147
leeks 140–142
preparing soil 31
taking plant out of pot 30
planting in ground 31
watering in 31
planting plans 132, 133
plot plans 132, 133
plums 170–174, 184
poles 9
cordons 127
frame for soft fruit 114, 125
staking 77
supporting netting 128
tepee 108–109
twiggy sticks 108
tying in 34
potting mix 12
acidic 12, 166, 167
digging in 15, 31, 152
drying out 41
general-purpose 12
handling 84
as mulch 76, 121
for planting out 31
propagation mix 12, 28, 29
window box 38
pollination 21
apple trees 120
by hand 92
self-pollination 175
wind 93
potassium 23, 45, 68
eggplant 148, 149
peppers 90, 91
strawberries 168
potato blight 81
potatoes 23
chitting 80
crop rotation 134
green 80, 81
growing in tub 78–81
hilling up 80, 81
planting plans 132, 133
storing 185
potbound plants 30
pots 10, 16–17
biodegradable 140
blueberries 164–167
eggplant 147
fruit trees in 116–121, 169
herbs 46
peppers 90
repotting pear tree 169
root crops 47
sowing seeds in 29, 84
slug protection 67
taking plant out of 30, 44
tomatoes 42–45
watering 32, 66
*see also* containers
preserves 184
propagation mix 12
propagator 11, 90, 146
pruners 9, 176, 179
pruning 174, 176–181
apples 120
basic 176–179
blueberries 167, 178
cherries 175
congested plants 176
cordons 127, 180
currants 125, 126
diseased plants 177
fig trees 121
gooseberries 127
pears 169
plums 173, 174
for productivity 178
raspberries 115, 178
shapes 180–181
pruning saw 177, 179
pumpkins 86, 135


## R


radishes 132, 134
growing in pot 47
rain barrels 32
rainwater 12, 32, 167
raised beds 14, 17
raspberries 185
fall 112–15
pruning 115, 178
summer 115
red currants 18, 133, 185
planting 126
repotting 73
reproduction 20–21
resistant varieties
carrots 97
gooseberries 127
leeks 143
root vegetables
crop rotation 134
growing in pots 47
storing 185
*see also individual types*
roots
root ball 118, 119, 166
root structure 23, 24
teasing out 119, 166
trimming 141
rosemary 51, 163
rot 13
garlic 58
leeks 143
onions 54
plum tree 172
stem rot 31
strawberries 62
zucchini seeds 84
rotation, crop 59
runner beans 19
growing up tepee 106–110
pests 109
sowing in pots 29, 108
staking 77
rutabagas 135, 185


## S


salad greens 36–39
growing in window box 36–39
lettuce 40
sand 13
deterring slugs 67
mixing tiny seeds with 38
sandy soil 13
seed bed 140
seed flats 10
cell packs 10, 102
replanting 30, 73
sowing in 28
taking plant out of 30
seedlings 66
pinching back 92
repotting 73
thinning out 40, 41
weeding 69
seeds
buying 28
collecting 28
germination 28, 38, 72
preventing rot 84
production 21
protecting 110
sowing in flats 28
sowing in furrows 72, 96
sowing in pots 29, 84, 90
sowing large seeds 29
sowing tiny seeds 28, 38
semidwarfs 181
shade 18, 176
currants 126
radishes 47
rhubarb 18
sheltered sites 19
shiny objects 129
sideshoots, pinching off 35, 45
slate chips 162, 163
slug collars 67

slug pellets 67
slugs and snails 65
protecting plants 67
runner beans 109, 110
salad greens 39
soaker hoses 33
soil 97, 125
adding leaf mold 137
clay 13, 160
free-draining 13, 50, 160
pH testing 14
preparing 15, 31, 152
sandy 13
storing carrots in 182–183
types 13
warming up 75
sowing seeds
cabbage 102
carrots 96
eggplant 146
in flats 28
in furrows 72
in gutters 111
indoors 28–29
in pots 29
larger seeds 29
leeks 140
outdoors 28
peppers 90
potting mix 12
salad in window box 38–39
sweet corn 93
tiny seeds 28, 38
zucchini 84
spade 8, 15
spinach 18, 132
bolting 41
crop rotation 134
growing in container 41
squashes 18, 93, 133
large 86
winter and summer 87
squirrels 128
staking 77
asparagus 153
eggplant 149
equipment 9
fruit trees 119, 172
peppers 91
sweet corn 93
tying in 34
stem rot 31
stomata 22, 24
stone chips 76
storing crops 184–185
carrots in soil 182–183
parsnips 99
straw mulch 76, 157
strawberries 132, 133
freezing 185
growing in container 17, 168
growing in basket 60–64
mulching 76
strawberry planter 168
sugar storage 23
sulfur chips 14, 115
sunlight 21, 22, 24
sunshine 18
supports
black currants 125
eggplant 148, 149
peas 111
raspberries 114
tepee 106–110, 167
tomatoes 44, 45
tying in 34
sweet corn 19, 133, 135
growing 93
Swiss chard 18, 41

## T

tepee 106–110, 167
thinning fruitlets 120
thinning out
cabbage 102
carrots 96
herbs 51
runner beans 108
salad greens 40, 41
seedlings 72
tomato blight 45, 65
tomato fertilizer 44, 45, 63, 65, 90, 120, 168
tomatoes 18, 133, 135
drying 184
feeding 68
green 45, 65
growing in basket 65
growing in pot 42–45
harvesting 45, 65
pinching back 35, 45
ripening 45, 65
supports 45, 77
trailing 44, 65
tying in 34, 45
tools, caring for 179
tote 10
training 86, 87, 180–181
gooseberries 127
tree ties 9, 119, 120, 172
trench, planting asparagus 152
trimming herbs 51, 162
tubs, potatoes in 80–81
turnips 98, 135
twiggy sticks 108, 167
twine 9, 34, 77, 108, 109
tying in 34, 45, 77

## V

ventilation
greenhouse 92
pruning 126, 176
straw mulch 76
thinning out 51
viola flowers 40

## W

wasps 64, 121, 174, 179
watering 32–33, 66
avoiding foliage 31, 32, 85, 103
before planting 46
black currants 124
cabbage 103
containers 16
eggplant 149
fruit trees 120, 121, 169, 173, 174
garlic 58
greenhouse 66
hanging baskets 51, 63
onion sets 54
overwatering 58, 59, 163
rainwater 12, 167
salad greens 39
sandy soils 13
sowing seeds 28, 29
spinach 41
strawberries 63, 64, 168
sweet corn 93
timing 32
tomatoes 45
window boxes 39, 41
zucchini in bags 85
watering in 31
watering can 8, 20–21, 22–23, 24–25, 31, 32, 51
weed-suppressing membrane 160, 163
weeding 69
asparagus 153
by hand 124
carrots 97
eggplant 149
garlic 58
leeks 143
onion sets 54
seedlings 69
soil preparation 15, 31, 69, 160
weeds 69, 76, 93
white currants 126
whiteflies 45
willow sticks 167
wind 19, 74
window boxes 10, 16, 39, 41
edible flowers 40
garlic 56
lettuce 40
salad greens 36–39
spinach 41
Swiss chard 41

## Z

zucchini 132, 133, 135
growing in bag 82–85

# About the Author

**Simon Akeroyd** is the Garden and Countryside Manager at Polesden Lacey in Surrey, UK, and was previously a Garden Manager for the Royal Horticultural Society. He has worked as a horticultural researcher and journalist for the BBC. He is the author of DK's *Simple Steps Lawns and Groundcover* and *Simple Steps Shrubs and Small Trees*, and the co-author of *Allotment Handbook* and *Grow Your Own Fruit*.

# Acknowledgments

## Photographic Credits

Dorling Kindersley would like to thank **Peter Anderson** for new photography.
**pp.18** (left); **105**; **128** (top); **129** (center): **Alan Buckingham** © Dorling Kindersley.
All other images © Dorling Kindersley.
For further information see
www.dkimages.com

## Publisher's Acknowledgments

Special thanks are due to **Squires Garden Centres** who kindly lent gardening tools for the photoshoots.
Dorling Kindersley would also like to thank:

**In the UK**
**Design assistance** Jessica Bentall, Alison Gardner, Elaine Hewson, Vicky Read
**DK Images** Claire Bowers, Freddie Marriage, Emma Shepherd, Romaine Werblow
**Indexer** Chris Bernstein

**In India**
**Design assistance** Ranjita Bhattacharji, Devan Das, Tanya Mehrotra, Ankita Mukherjeel
**Senior Art Editor** Ivy Roy
**Editorial assistance** Swati Mittal
**Senior Editor** Garima Sharma
**DTP Designers** Rajesh Singh Adhikari, Sourabh Chhallaria, Arjinder Singh
**CTS/DTP Manager** Sunil Sharma

**At Tall Tree Ltd**
**Editor** Rob Colson
**Designer** Malcolm Parchment